Getting Started
A Practical Guide To House Church Planting

Compiled by Felicity Dale

Acknowledgements:

Unless otherwise indicated, all Scripture quotations are taken from the *Holy Bible*, New Living Translation, copyright © 1996. Used by permission of Tyndale House Publishers, Inc., Wheaton, Illinois 60189. All rights reserved.

Scripture quotations noted NKJV are from the *Holy Bible*, New King James Version. Copyright © 1979, 1980, 1982, 1990, 1994 by Thomas Nelson, Inc.

Using this Study Guide

The layout of the material is served up in two-page format.

The left-hand page contains the main body of the teaching material, with practical application ideas in the left margin. The right-hand page contains information that amplifies or illustrates the teaching material.

Contents

INTRODUCTION

Bob, excited after reading his first issue of House2House Magazine, takes his first step in changing his house into a house church.

On the Cover:

We all recognize that it would be ludicrous to think nailing a steeple to the roof of a house would make it a house church. However, many of us take what we've seen happen in church buildings our whole lives and duplicate it in our living room and call it a church. House church is not really about a change of location, it's about a change in the way we do church.

This reason for this manual is simple. At the House2House office, we were getting inundated with requests for help in starting simple or house churches. We decided the easiest way to help would be to write something from our experience.

This manual is not intended to provide a methodology nor a model for church planting. Neither is it comprehensive. It is a collection of ideas taken from our own experience, and the experiences of others who have already done it. Hopefully, you will be able to avoid some of the mistakes that all of us made! There are an abundance of examples from here in Austin and from our times in India. By sharing from our own experience, we are sure that the examples are reasonably accurate and not hyped!

The first part of the manual is more theoretical. For those who are only interested in the more practical side, I suggest starting at Section 8. However, I would request that at some stage you go back and read the sections on the Great Commission and prayer.

Our prayer is that God would transform this nation through a movement of ordinary people with a passion to see His Kingdom come, who will lay down their lives for the sake of seeing the lost brought into life-transforming communities of His people.

The mission statement of House2House is that "we are pursuing the rapid advancement of the Kingdom of God by saturating and transforming communities with radical, home-based, church planting movements."

Jesus did not leave us with a model to build, but a guide to follow. We experience the life of the church not because we meet a certain way or in a certain place, but because we learn to listen to God together and let Him teach us how to share His life. If we substitute any method or design for that process, we will end up following it instead of Him and building a counterfeit instead of the real deal.

Wayne Jacobsen, *Bodylife* Feb 2002

GOD WANTS YOU

Throughout the world, God is using people just like you to start churches. Businessmen and housewives, senior citizens and children, illiterates and PhD's (but many more illiterates), are being used by God as His servants to extend His Kingdom. His people are on Kingdom assignment to make disciples. Jesus is building His church!

No longer is starting churches reserved for those who have gone through years of seminary training. No longer is it only the task of those with the title of pastor. No longer is it only the privilege of those with a special anointing. The Holy Spirit is not limited by our lack of natural ability or experience. All God is looking for is a willing, servant heart and someone who will listen to Him and follow as He leads.

If you are willing, God will use you. God wants you. The question is . . . ARE YOU WILLING?

- A customer service manager in Texas starts two groups at his office and another across town

- An Indian housewife starts fifty churches in one year

- A PhD graduate in Madras, India and his 13-year-old son start a church with a street vendor

- An 85-year-old lady, from a group in a retirement center, leads a group in an assisted living community

- In Nepal, children as young as 9 or 10 are being used to start churches.

WHAT IS YOUR EXCUSE?

Practical Application:
Can you gather two or three people together to study this manual with you, and to join you in praying towards starting churches in your area?

I remember in Los Angeles, at the beginning of the AD 2000 movement, there was a group of us from around the world sharing about what God was doing. Then someone asked the question, "What do you think God wants to do on your continent?" And everybody shared about the big revivals that God wanted to bring. Then the next question was, "Tell us the three things that you believe make that impossible." And it was amazing! People from each continent got up to state the reasons why the things they know God wants to do, will not be possible! The North American group stood up first and said, "It will not be possible because we don't have unity, we don't have vision and we don't have money." The Europeans got up and said, "We're confused. We don't have vision. We don't have unity." The people from Russia stood up and said, "We have this KGB mentality—never to tell the whole truth. Hiding back because we know truth is power. And we don't have money or vision." And it went around the world, a wailing cry. But then someone else stood up. He was a math teacher from Nigeria who started a little home group in 1974, which grew into a church of 120,000 in the Sunday morning service, and they had already planted roughly 4,500 churches. He stood up and said, "In Africa we don't have all these problems you have described. In Africa we have only one problem, and it stands right in front of your nose. I am the problem. You have to pray for me with my small vision that I will not stand in the way of God's big vision. I with my great plan will not stand in the way of God's greater plan. I with my small dreams will not stand in the way of God's dream for not only me, but for the nations! Pray, therefore, that this problem shall be solved. The only real way is through the cross."

Wolfgang Simson

"So, laying eggs all the time and then getting plucked, stuffed, and roasted is good enough for you, is it?"

"It's a living!"

"You know what the problem is? The fences aren't just around the farm. They're up here." (Pointing to his head)

Chicken Run, the movie

THE BIG PICTURE

From all over the world, we are hearing the stories. Our hearts are stirred by descriptions of major moves of the Holy Spirit, where tens of thousands are being swept into the Kingdom and churches are multiplying on a daily basis.

We have personally had the privilege of seeing some of these movements first hand. In Mozambique, the poorest of all nations, Rolland and Heidi Baker are caught up in a move of God's Spirit. From the humblest beginnings, they now have an orphanage where over a thousand children have been rescued from a life of abject poverty on the streets or the city refuse dump. Over 3000 churches have been started over the past 5 years in Mozambique and neighboring countries. It was an unforgettable experience to spend two or three days in a village doing medical work and preaching the gospel, and to leave behind a church of 50 to 100 new Christians, who would be followed up by one of the pastors that Rolland and Heidi had trained.

In India, we had the opportunity of spending time with a church planter who has seen over 3000 churches start since 1993. When asked what he considers a church, he will gently explain that, to keep the numbers down, they now consider a group to be a church only if they have at least 3 families that have been baptized, are led by indigenous leadership and have already planted at least one other church! We estimate that there are approximately 100,000 that have become Christians in this movement.

This is happening on a worldwide scale. In *Church Planting Movements*, by David Garrison, the Southern Baptists report the following:

> **Southeast Asia**
> *When a Southern Baptist strategy coordinator began his assignment in 1993, there were only three churches and 85 believers among a popula-*

Lino is intense. His eyes are wide and lit up, his hands are waving and gesturing. He turns and shifts excitedly. He can't be quieted. He knows what he's talking about, and he sounds like it. He speaks with authority, and I am listening, taking down every detail. I hit him with every question I can think of, and he answers me transparently, effortlessly. He has been raised from the dead, and I want to know all about it.

Pastor Lino Andrade is one of our more than one thousand pastors in Mozambique. His mud hut church is in the town of Gondola in the central province of Manica, not far from Chimoio where we have had major conferences. He has just begun a three-month Bible school term with us at our Zimpeto center in southern Mozambique. Today he testified in church, and now I am with him face-to-face, getting every bit of information I can.

This morning he declared earnestly to all our children, staff and Bible school students that life after death is real, the supernatural world is real, angels are real, and the power of Jesus is real. He should know. He is one of about ten people in our churches who have been brought from death back to life by the Author of life, and we want to tell everyone!

Lino is a widower, and he stays with his daughter in her little house in Gondola. Not long before coming down for Bible school, he got seriously sick. He couldn't eat or sleep. He was in great pain. Too poor for medical attention, he didn't know what was wrong. Over the course of a month he kept deteriorating until he died. Instead of burying him, his daughter called for Pastor Joni, also in Gondola, who came with four other church leaders to pray. Lino's eyes were rolled back into his head, and his body soon began to smell of decay. But Jesus has used Joni to raise the dead before, and Joni was determined.

(continued on page 11)

tion of more than 7 million. Four years later, there were more than 550 churches and nearly 55,000 believers.

India
One elderly man, who came to Christ in a church planting movement, planted 42 churches in his first year as a believer.

North Africa
In his weekly Friday sermon, an Arab Muslim cleric complained that more than 10,000 Muslims, living in the surrounding mountains, had apostatized from Islam and become Christians.

City in China
Over a four-year period (1993-1997), more than 20,000 people came to faith in Christ, resulting in more than 500 new churches.

Western Europe
A missionary in Europe reports: "Last year (1998), my wife and I started 15 new church cell groups. As we left for a six-month stateside assignment last July, we wondered what we'd find when we returned. It's wild! We can verify at least 30 churches now, but I believe that it could be two or even three times that many."

Ethiopia
A missionary strategist commented, "It took us 30 years to plant four churches in this country. We've started 65 cell churches in the last nine months."

Every region of the world now pulsates with some kind of **church planting movement**. Sometimes we see only the numbers, but often they are accom-

Prayer Point:
According to research by George Barna, there is not one county in the United States that is currently experiencing overall growth in the number of Christians.

(continued from page 9)

Lino was released from his body and given a vision of what might be. He watched his own funeral procession, and could see others lowering his own casket into the ground. He watched them put flowers on his grave. Two bright angels with wings came to him. He was shown things that have not yet been explained to him. But in the vision, Lino refused to accept his own death. And then he heard God tell him that he was not going to heaven yet, but that he had many more years to live. In his spirit, he could hear Joni praying loudly and fervently.

After a few hours, he returned to his body and awoke in bed, but was very weak and nauseous from his own smell. Satan did not get his way, and Lino was not buried. Lino gradually got his strength back, and his body normalized as everyone around looked after him. His church and all who knew him were incredibly encouraged. Lino himself is now strong and bold, always eager to minister.

Lino is an example of what happens when the poor, sick and desperate get close to Jesus. They want Him. They know they need Him, all the time and in every way. And if He can raise the dead, He can certainly take care of hunger, poverty and every other problem and affliction. We didn't come to Africa just to feed some children and give out a few clothes. We came to bring the wretched and forgotten close to Him, in the worst of circumstances. And we came to see what He can do when He draws close to them in return. Everything changes. All things are possible. The Word is true. Our Jesus can save to the uttermost. And all of us, all over the world, have hope who trust in Him.

Jesus has encouraged us in many ways recently. One lady's lungs were completely restored after she nearly died of advanced pneumonia. A man living in a shack near the dump, paralyzed from the waist down for two years, immediately rose to his feet and walked after baptism and prayer. A lady who for twenty-one years was totally blind in one eye and very blurry in the other can see clearly out of both. So, many wanted to testify last Sunday in church along with Pastor Lino that we had to ask them to stop and continue later. Two young men from the dump are now in our Bible school. Many of our pastors are receiving visions. One of our strongest preachers is a fourteen-year-old boy up north, with a powerful evangelistic call. Healings follow him everywhere he goes.

Rolland Baker, *Reporting what God is doing in Mozambique*

panied by lively descriptions, such as this recently received e-mail message: "All of our cell churches have lay pastors/leaders, because we turn over the work so fast that the missionary seldom leads as many as two or three Bible studies before God raises at least one leader. The new leader seems to be both saved and called to lead at the same time, so we baptize him and give him a Bible. After the new believers/leaders are baptized, they are so on fire that we simply cannot hold them back. They fan out all over the country starting Bible studies, and, a few weeks later, we begin to get word back on how many have started. It's the craziest thing we ever saw! We did not start it, and we couldn't stop it if we tried."

But what about the West? Can God do this here, or do we have to be content to sit wistfully on the sidelines, watching the action in the arena of the rest of the world? At House2House, we are in a very privileged position because we are contacted by people on a daily basis telling us how God is using them to start new churches. We may not yet have the incredible numbers that other countries do, but the initial droplets have become a trickle, and that will turn into a stream and eventually into a mighty, roaring torrent! Do it, Lord!!

Seen from a historical perspective, God is at work recovering His bride, the church. From His original blueprint in the book of Acts, the church rapidly slid downhill. The New Testament church was a dynamic, living organism where every person had significance and took an active role. They mostly met in homes, sharing their lives together on a daily basis. It was more a lifestyle than a series of meetings or teachings. However, under the Emperor Constantine, Christianity became the state religion, and a number of changes took place, while the church joined the rest of society going into what became known historically as the "Dark Ages."

So, what is a Church Planting Movement? A simple, concise definition of a Church Planting Movement (CPM) is a rapid and multiplicative increase of indigenous churches planting churches within a given people group or population segment.

David Garrison, *Church Planting Movements*

"The continued growth of Christian churches (mostly underground house churches) in China has something to do with three convictions widespread among Chinese Christians. The Chinese love the progression "good, better, best" so the three mottoes are "It is good for a Christian to lead someone to Christ. It is better to plant a church. It is best to start a church-planting movement."

Indian Christians have three similar convictions: "Every Christian can plant a church; every house can become a church; every church can become a Bible school."

John White

After Pentecost, the early believers gathered in both the temple courts and in homes (Acts 2:46; 5:42). As the gospel spread out from Jerusalem to new regions and peoples, gatherings in homes became the normative practice (Rom 16:5; 1 Cor 16:19; Col 4:15). These early believers also shared a larger, united identity as the *ekklesia* of the city (e.g. Corinth - 1 Cor 14:23; 11:18) or the church of a region (e.g. Galatia - Gal 1:1-2; c.f. Acts 15:41; 18:23). It seems that these home churches would occasionally gather as a larger expression of the people of God (1 Cor 11:18; 14:23). This dual pattern of church in the home and church of the city would continue for three more centuries until Constantine institutionalized the church.

Jonathan Campbell, *The Translatability of Christian Community*

Originally, Roman persecution had caused the Church to grow in numbers. But in AD 313 Emperor Constantine issued the Edict of Milan, which ended that. Endorsed from the throne, Christianity very shortly became so identified with the Empire that everyone born in it was automatically considered "Christian." Membership in the church became attractive for worldly reasons. And, as a direct result of the influence of the Romans upon the Church, Europe entered into the period of history we now call the Dark Ages.

Following the traditions of the pagan religions at that time, Constantine built temples for the Christians to meet in. Plato's influence again loomed in the use of stained glass windows, lofty steeples, and high, vaulted church ceilings. All of these were designed to reach toward the presence of the "unknowable" God. James Rutz's book, The Open Church, *also points out that a paid, professional clergy arose during this time. The clergy-lay distinction, so predominant today, was officially sanctioned by the fourth century church. The Biblical mandate for the priesthood of all believers was ignored. Christians became spectators, lulled into allowing professionals to approach the Almighty on their behalf. The Dark Ages fell upon them quickly.*

It was dark–for a very long time.

Mike and Sue Dowgiewicz, *The Prodigal Church*

From the earliest times, men have attempted to reform the church. Some, like the early apostles, lost their lives. Others, like Luther and Calvin, effected significant theological and cultural changes.

It wasn't until the Edict of Milan in 313 AD that the emperor Constantine began to actually favor Christians. At this point, a number of seemingly positive, but in reality negative, things began to take place. Clergy were exempted from taxation (319 AD); the church was given the right to be seen as a corporation (although not in our present-day sense); Sunday work was forbidden to city-dwellers; gifts were made to clergy; the Roman eagle on standards (flags, banners and ensigns) was replaced with the sign of Christ, and large, religious buildings were built (in Rome, Jerusalem, Bethlehem, etc.). These things were positive on the surface since it was a 180 degree turn from persecutions over the previous years. They were negative in that they reinforced some of the harmful practices which began to creep into the church during the 100 years or so prior.

Robert Lund, The Way Church Ought To Be

It is interesting to note that from the period of 400 AD to even this present day there were groups of Christians who were routinely branded heretics, that would not bow their knee to the ruling religious body. In some cases, this would be the Roman Catholic Church; in others it might be the Lutheran Church or even others yet. The point being, God always preserved small groups of believers that would carry the torch of the testimony of Christianity. This torch represented the elements of simple and pure Christianity that Paul so carefully warned the brethren at Corinth to guard.

Over the next one thousand years, the church, in the global sense, went into sort of an ice age, spiritually speaking. Kenneth Scott Latourette says of this time: "The main outlines of the Christianity of the year 500, even though altered in details, continued to be the chief characteristics of the Christianity of the year 1500 . . . More specifically, this age shows what happens when we mix spiritual weapons, principles, ideas, wisdom, structures, and practices with those that are humanly logical, earthly, religious, and carnal . . . Instead of the church rising up with the tools which were part of the Christian's toolbox, she resorted to politics, warfare, torture, intimidation, deceit, false doctrine, and a myriad of other anti-Scriptural methods in order to 'expand' the Kingdom of God."

Robert Lund, The Way Church Ought To Be

THE BIG PICTURE

Arthur Wallis, the elder statesman of the New Churches in Britain, gave a masterful explanation of church development over the centuries in his introduction to the book, Another Wave Rolls In. His analogy of the onward flow of the Holy Spirit's work through the church being like the incoming tide is powerful. What energy! What beauty and awesome power is displayed as the waves crash against the rocks. Nothing can stand in their way. Each wave represents a new truth unveiled that the church grasps. With the Reformation, that truth was salvation by faith. With the Baptists, it was the importance of baptism by full immersion that came to the forefront. With the Pentecostals, the baptism in the Holy Spirit was once again brought to the attention of the whole body of Christ. God is progressively revealing (bringing new light from the timeless scriptures) truth so that He will have His way in His church, and one day His Bride will be without spot or blemish (Eph. 5:26).

Tony and Felicity Dale, *Simply Church*

But, none of these movements made any change to the way the church is structured.

However, now we see God emphasizing fundamental changes in the way that church is run. On every continent, church planting movements are springing up that are primarily based in small groups, whether that be homes, offices, factories, schools or wherever people spend time together. They are lay led, the distinction between clergy and laity having vanished. They are aggressively evangelistic, with new converts quickly being discipled, and then, in turn, sent out to start new churches themselves. There is little formality. The times together, frequently based around a meal, are organic and free-flowing, specifically

The Reformation was a great start on fixing what was wrong with the church, but it fell far short in regard to structures and practice. It succeeded marvelously in getting back to sound doctrine: sola Scriptura (placing the Bible over church tradition), sola gratia (salvation by grace), and sola fide (through faith, not works). But the Reformation never got us back to the first century pattern of meeting that we see in Paul's letters. It simply exchanged the priest for a minister and put a sermon in place of the Eucharist.

James Rutz, *The Open Church*

meeting the needs of the people gathered together. Everyone has an active part to play – no one is merely a spectator! To quote a recent talk by a church leader in India:

> *This is a special period of apostolic grace for India. Everything we call church is changing. The church is changing from pastoral ministries to apostolic and prophetic ministries. The church is changing from Sunday services to everyday worship.   The church is changing from one-man shows to every-person royal priesthood. God said, "I will pour out My Spirit on all flesh, on men and women, young and old, everyone."*
>
> *Hallelujah! Big changes are taking place. Church is changing from a single worship building to every house being a house of God. Church is changing from congregational models to house church models, from large congregations to "where two or three are gathered together in my name, I am present there." Church is changing from a traditional worship pattern to an open system. In 1 Corinthians 14:26, the original Greek word translated "everyone" is used three times. Everyone participates. It is a participating church.*

Another wave is coming in. And, as the Priceline.com ad says, "This one is going to be big—really big!" What is happening to the church worldwide could be as far-reaching as the Reformation.

Dawn Ministries (Discipling A Whole Nation), has the vision of a church within walking distance of every person on the planet. This translates to a Great Commission church that is actively reaching out into the community, for every 500 to 1000 people. In the Philippines twenty-five years ago, they estimated they

. . . The catalyst for this new reformation will be the people, not the professionals. Other changes must occur as well. While it is true that certain things cannot and must not change —for example, the Bible has been and always will be the standard for the church—there are some significant transitions that will have to take place in the emerging church:

Change factor:	Changing from:	Changing to:
Authority	centralized	decentralized
Leadership	pastor-driven	lay-driven
Power distribution	vertical	horizontal
Reaction to change	resistance	acceptance
Identity	tradition and order	mission and vision
Scope of ministry	all-purpose	specialized
Practices	tradition bound	relevance bound
People's role	observation and support	participation and innovation
Principle product	knowledge	transformation
Success factors	size, efficiency, image	accessibility, impact, integrity
Effect of technology	attention-grabbing	growth-facilitating
Means to growth	more, better-run programs	relationships and experiences
Growth prospects	limited	unlimited

George Barna, *The Second Coming of the Church*

Practical Application:
How many Great Commission churches would your neighborhood or city need to fulfill the vision of a church for every 1000 people?

Practical Application:
1). Watch the video *Church Planting Movements*

2). Read the booklet *Church Planting Movements* by David Garrison.

(These are available to order from the Southern Baptist International Mission Board website, www.imb.org)

would need at least 50,000 churches to fulfill that vision. As they talked to churches that already existed, mission organizations as well as their own workers in the field, the idea took hold. Now they have exceeded their goal with over 60,000 churches having been planted!

What would that mean here in the West? Austin has a population of around 1 million. Could we dare to believe God for 1000 churches in this city? Every neighborhood, apartment complex, university dorm, retirement center etc. would have at least one church.

Recently the challenge has gone out for Christians to aim for one million house churches here in the States. Some people object to the emphasis on numbers, saying that quality is what we should be going for. But translate that into transformed lives and communities!

I love to body surf in the ocean (never having mastered the genuine sport where you actually stand up on the board!) When you surf, you are out there in the water waiting for the big one, the wave that you can catch at exactly the right moment just as it is starting to break. The others you let go by. And then you see it coming in the distance, and you know it is your wave. As it reaches you, you paddle for all you are worth, and if you have caught it right, it will carry you all the way in to the shore.

This wave of house church or simple church Christianity is our wave. It is just at the point where we can launch ourselves forward as it rolls in. Right now is the time to paddle for all we're worth, and we're in for the ride of a lifetime.

A case in point is the different reproduction patterns of elephants and rabbits:

Elephants

Only fertile four times a year

Only one baby per pregnancy

22-month gestation period

Sexual maturity: 18 years

Maximum growth potential in 3 years: from 2 elephants to 3

Rabbits

Almost continuously fertile

Average of seven babies per pregnancy

1-month gestation period

Sexual maturity: 4 months

Maximum growth potential in 3 years: from 2 rabbits to 476 million

Wolfgang Simson, *Houses that Change the World*

WHAT IS CHURCH?

House church Christianity is the body of Christ in an ordinary house. In many ways a house church is like a spiritual, extended family: relational, spontaneous and organic. For its everyday life, the organization, bureaucracy and ceremonies of a house church need not be much different than that of a typical large family.

The house church reflects God's qualities and character. This community lifestyle is molded in the spirit of love, truth, forgiveness, faith and grace. House churches are the way we love each other, forgive each other, mourn with those who mourn and laugh with those who laugh, extend and receive grace and constantly remain in touch with God's truth and forgiveness. It is a place where all masks can fall, and we can be open to each other and still keep loving each other.

Wolfgang Simson, *Houses that Change the World*

Churches that embody the values of simple or house church Christianity meet in all sorts of places. They meet in offices, hospitals, retirement centers, factories, homes, under trees, and even in church buildings! Equally, meeting in a home does not prevent us from being at least as traditional as the church that meets in the building with the spire. In many ways it is a shame that this movement is known as the "house-church movement" because it somehow gives the impression that the only Scriptural way to meet is in homes!

So why do we believe in getting together the way that we do? What are the values that characterize this type of Christianity, wherever the Christians may meet?

Where do you go to church? I have never liked this question, even when I was able to answer it with a specific organization. I know what it means culturally, but it is based on a false premise—that church is something you can go to as in a specific event, location or organized group. I think Jesus looks at the church quite differently. He didn't talk about it as a place to go to, but a way of living in relationship to Him and others in His family. Asking me where I go to church is like asking me where I go to Jacobsen. How do I answer that? I am a Jacobsen and where I go Jacobsen is. "Church" is that kind of word. It doesn't identify a location or an institution. It describes a people and how they relate to each other.

Wayne Jacobsen, *Why I Don't Go To Church Anymore*

. . .Meeting in homes is no cure-all. I've been to some very sick home meetings and met in facilities with groups who shared an authentic body life together. But the time I spend in regular body life I want to spend face to face with hungry people who are being transformed by Jesus.

Wayne Jacobsen, *Why I Don't Go To Church Anymore*

The strength of a nation lies in the homes of its people.

Abraham Lincoln

WHAT IS CHURCH?

Today, we talk about the church in a number of different ways.

- A building

- A small group, such as a cell or house church

- A congregation - First Baptist Church, or New Life Fellowship

- The church in a location, e.g. the church in Austin, the church in Latin America

- A denomination like the Catholics or Baptists

- The church universal

It is interesting that in Scripture we only see the term "church" used in the following ways:

- The church that meets in a person's house e.g., the church that meets in Priscilla and Aquila's house (Romans 16:4)

- The church in a location e.g., the church in Jerusalem (Acts 15:4) or the churches in a province such as Galatia (Galatians 1:2)

- The church universal i.e., all believers everywhere throughout the ages (Ephesians 1:22,23)

Jesus Himself is only recorded as talking about the church on two occasions. The first is in Matthew 16 after Peter's great declaration of faith, "You are the Messiah, the Son of the living God." Jesus' response to this is, "You are Peter, and on this rock I will build My church, and the gates of Hades shall not prevail against it"(NKJV). This must refer to the church universal.

Then in Matthew 18, when discussing how to handle sin in the life of a believer, Jesus says that if the person who is sinning will not listen when you go to him with a witness, then you are

However, a church was not a congregation of 5000, 2000 or even 200. Rather, the New Testament church was a fellowship of smaller churches. This didn't mean that if there were twenty or thirty churches in a city that the church was fractured. The Apostle Paul often referred to the church in a city or region as one church—such as the church in Corinth. It was one church even though it met in many different places. Although Paul knew of various local churches in a city, he wrote one letter with the assumption that it would suffice for all the churches in the area. This dual pattern of church, or inter-church dependance, would continue for three more centuries until Constantine centralized Christianity through the institutionalization of the church.

These two expressions of church—local and city—facilitated the extensive growth and reproduction of the early church throughout the Roman world (cf. Acts 2:42ff; 5:42; 20:20). In the most basic sense, the church is an assembly of believers who are united together around the Lordship of Jesus Christ.

Jonathan Campbell, *The Translatability of Christian Community*

The Greek word for church, *ekklesia*, is composed of two words: "ek" meaning "out of," and "kalleo," meaning "I call." The full and simple meaning of "church" according to the original word is, "I call out from." When Jesus said, "I will build my church," He was saying, "I will call My people out of the world, and they will assemble in My name, and the gates of Hell shall not prevail against them." This implies that His called-out people will rally as an army to take the world for Him, and the enemy will not be able to stop the advance. This invincible army will be motivated by the love of God within their hearts and a message of God's love and forgiveness on their lips.

Actually, *ekklesia* carries two concepts: being called out and being assembled together. We cannot experience church until we come together.

Robert Fitts, *Saturation Church Planting*

WHAT IS CHURCH?

to *take it to the church*. It goes on, "Whatever you prohibit on earth is prohibited in heaven, and whatever you allow on earth is allowed in heaven…If two of you agree down here on earth concerning anything you ask, My Father in heaven will do it for you. For where two or three are gathered together because they are mine, I am there among them." This is obviously a local body of believers. **Many take that last sentence, "Where two or three are gathered in My name, I am there among them," to be the simplest definition of church.**

In Acts 2 we see that in the very first days of the church, "all the believers met together constantly and shared everything they had…They worshipped together at the Temple each day, met in homes for the Lord's Supper, and shared their meals with great joy and generosity – all the while praising God and enjoying the goodwill of all the people."

So we see that from the day of Pentecost, the new believers in Jerusalem met together in homes as well as in the temple. After the martyrdom of Stephen, the disciples were forcibly dispersed, traveling far and wide preaching the gospel. From this point on, apart from the mention of a meeting place in the Hall of Tyrranus, church is expressed in two ways; church that takes place in a home, and the church of a geographical area. This pattern of meeting in homes continued for just under three hundred years.

What is going on now? Throughout the world God is blessing in traditional and cell churches of every description, as well as the house church movements. Within many of the traditional and cell-based models of church, we see the Holy Spirit nudging people towards something more organic, based on smaller groups. All three models of church need to be working together to advance the Kingdom of God in any way that they can.

Prayer Point:
It is estimated that worldwide there are approximately…

•450 million Christians within traditional, congregational models,

•10 million in cell-based churches, and

•450 million in simple, organic structures such as house churches, or meeting outdoors.

When two or three true, born-again believers come together in His name, Jesus is in the midst. Jesus in the midst is church! It is a different experience than Jesus within. We cannot experience Jesus in the midst when we are alone. We can only experience Jesus in the midst when we are in company with others—at least one or two others.

But is it a church in the fullest sense of the word? Yes, it is a church in the fullest sense of the word. It is the basic church. You can have more than two or three and it is still a church, but it does not become "more church" because there are more than two or three. It only becomes a bigger church.

Robert Fitts, *Saturation Church Planting*

This sort of Christianity is infectious; it is generous; it is full of grace and mercy. It allows others to be different from us; it allows other churches to create different models and be different from our own. It means we have less to criticize because in the final analysis we are asking important questions about the fruit in people's lives, our effectiveness in reaching out to the lost, and quality of life that allows us to be signs and symbols. In previous ages, holy things were wrapped up in religious paraphernalia. Today we don't need many signs and symbols—we are the signs and symbols.

Gerald Coates, *Non-Religious Christianity*

Christians may not always see eye to eye, but they can walk arm in arm.

Unknown

WHAT IS CHURCH?

Why house church? There are a number of reasons:

1. It does appear that through most of the New Testament, the primary meeting place was in homes. When the apostles preached in the synagogue, it usually did not take long before they were thrown out. And there are frequent references to the church in a person's home. Archeological evidence from New Testament times also confirms this (although occasionally the houses were modified).

2. It is difficult to obey the commands of the New Testament in groups that get too large. A very instructive study is to look up the fifty-four 'one anothers' of the New Testament (See Appendix 1). We are told to bear one another's burdens (Galatians 6:2), to admonish one another (Colossians 3:16), to confess our sin to one another (James 5:16). These are next to impossible in a larger context.

3. In I Corinthians chapters 11 - 14, the only specific instructions as to how meetings are to be conducted are given. I Corinthians 14:26 says that when we come together each person should be able to bring a contribution, whether it be a song, a teaching, etc. This would only be possible in a smaller setting.

4. It takes too long to build a building and train a pastor, if we are to ever see rapid growth of the church. The Southern Baptists estimate that it takes $320,000 to start a new church, if you include the building, the pastor's training and his first year's salary! House churches can multiply at negligible cost and at a very rapid rate. This has been demonstrated in many countries.

5. This is clearly something that God is doing in this generation throughout the world. It is a part of His restoration of the Body of Christ. The wave is coming, so let's get ready.

Practical Application:
Study together with your group what happened in homes in the New Testament. Can you find the following:

1). Miracles

2). Prayer times

3). Meetings

4). Communion

5). Baptisms

Here are some great electronic Bible search tools:

www.crosswalk.com

www.biblegateway.com

First, emphasize house churches. When the church begins to grow in cities among non-Christians, each congregation must soon find a place to assemble. The congregation should meet in the most natural surroundings, to which non-Christians can come with the greatest ease and where the converts themselves carry on the services. Obtaining a place to assemble should not lay a financial burden on the little congregation. The house church meets all these requirements ideally. House churches should always be considered, both for initial planting and for later extension.

Dr. Donald McGavran, *Understanding Church Growth*

The house church has emerged as yet another model vying for people's participation. The house church appeals to Americans because it fits our culture. It is decentralized, has a horizontal structure, exerts low control and authority over its participants, and operates without historical traditions. House churches offer convenience in scheduling and location, are highly relational, and do not waste money on buildings and overhead. They represent the ultimate in flexibility.

George Barna, *The Second Coming of the Church*

In the early days, Christianity was considered a strange religion because it didn't have buildings. That was one of the reasons it was so feared and disliked. Not only did the Christians have allegiance to a different King, but they could be anywhere. They "infiltrated" the entire nation—right down to Caesar's own household—and spread their message like wildfire.

Juanita and Johnny Berguson, *Whatever Happened to Christianity*

If you had asked another for directions to a church in any important city of the first century world, you would have been directed to somebody's home!

Del Birkey, *The House Church*

The house church, more than any other model, is best prepared.....because it is informal, relational, mobile, not financially encumbered with overhead costs, and is easily planted in a variety of settings. Also, it reproduces faster and spreads farther because it can be a decentralized approach to a region, nation, or people group, and is not dependent upon heavily-trained clergy.

Neil Cole and Paul Kaak, *Organic Church Planting*

HOUSE CHURCH DNA

What then are the values on which simple or house church Christianity is built? If we are to see a rapid multiplication of churches across this nation, what is the essential DNA that needs to permeate every cell of the body? This list is by no means exhaustive. For the sake of space we are not covering basic issues such as the importance of obedience to the Word of God, or the essential nature of prayer. The following are not covered in any particular order of priority.

1.   Christ is the head of the church

Jesus wants His church back! Let's give the Lord the headship of His church (Ephesians 4:15,16). Let's give Him sovereign authority over His body. Let's expect Him to say to us prophetically, "I want you to make disciples in that apartment complex," and for us to obey. Let's yield the direction and control in our meetings to the Holy Spirit and watch in awe as He orchestrates according to His divine plan for us. Let's anticipate that He will give us gifts of knowledge and healing and that we will see the supernatural happening in the market place, as "the Word becomes flesh and dwells among us." Let us go to battle against the principalities and powers and let's see captives set free in the name of Jesus. Lord, build Your church!

2.   The priesthood of all believers

I Peter 2:9 declares that we are a kingdom of priests and God's holy nation. All of us are priests. **The New Testament church knew nothing of a distinction between clergy and laity.** That did not come into being until the church had been in existence for a couple of centuries. In New Testament times everyone was expected to take a role. Every member of the body was important, and each had a vital part to play for the body to work effectively. (I Corinthians 12:12-27, Romans 12:4-8)

What does this mean for us? First, there are no areas that are off limits to Mr. Average Christian (if there is such a thing!) Baptism? If you lead someone to the Lord, then go ahead and

Practical Application:
Group Question: How do we let the Lord be more in charge of our times together?

Individual Question: How do I make a decision between two good choices? How do I hear God's voice?

Jesus Christ has today almost no authority at all among the groups that call themselves by His name.

Among the gospel churches, Christ is now in fact little more than a beloved symbol. "All Hail the Power of Jesus' Name" is the church's national anthem and the cross is her official flag, but in the week-by-week services of the church and the day-by-day conduct of her members, someone else, not Christ, makes the decisions.

In the conduct of our public worship where is the authority of Christ to be found? The truth is that today the Lord rarely controls a service, and the influence He exerts is very small. We sing of Him and preach about Him, but He must not interfere; we worship our way, and it must be right because we have always done it that way.

For the true Christian, the supreme test for the present soundness and ultimate worth of everything religious must be the place our Lord occupies in it. Is He Lord or symbol? Is He in charge of the project or merely one of the crew? Does He decide things or only help to carry out the plans of others? All religious activities may be proved by the answer to the question: Is Jesus Christ Lord in this act?

A.W. Tozer, *The Waning Authority of Christ in the Churches*

In regard to church-planting patterns, external human control over the new converts and churches is inversely proportional to the potential growth and rate of growth in terms of both maturity and size.

A friend from China

There are many errors that have come to the church where headship or government is given to somebody other than Christ. The house church movement believes in headship. It is not the headship of an authoritarian or autocratic leadership, or a requirement to submit to leadership simply because of position or office. It is recognition that "the head of the body is Christ" (Col. 2:19) and that people who are the church are to "grow up into all things into Him who is the head—Christ" (Eph 4:15).

Derek Brown

baptize them (Acts 8:38). Communion? Nowhere does it say that it takes a special person to share the bread and wine with others. (The Lord's supper of the New Testament church was part of a larger meal, but that is a different subject!) Praying for the sick? That is also for every believer (Mark 16:19).

This is not to say that people will not have different roles or that there will not be leadership. It is obvious that both functioned in the early church. However, there is much more emphasis on the importance of every member ministering. Those with a special function, such as apostles and prophets, clearly ministered as part of the body. Decisions were often made corporately (Acts 15:22). Frank Viola writes:

> Take, for instance, Corinth, the most troubled church in the NT. Throughout the entire Corinthian correspondence, Paul never appeals to the elders. He never chastises them. He never commends obedience to them. In fact, he does not even mention them!

> Instead, Paul appeals to the whole church. He shows that it is her responsibility to deal with her own (the church's) self-inflicted wounds. Paul charges and implores "the brethren" over thirty times in I Corinthians. He writes as if no officers exist. This is true for all his other letters to churches in crisis.

> Notice that Paul's stress is on function, not on position. His stress is also placed upon the whole church. For the entire book of Corinthians is a plea to the entire assembly to handle its own problems.

One of the main ways that the priesthood of all believers will work itself out is in open style meetings where anyone can take part and the Holy Spirit is in charge of the agenda. A whole section will be devoted to this subject later.

Almost every great movement trickles up, not down. The revolution of faith will not be sparked by the institutions and high-profile leaders who publicly represent the Christian church today . . . The movement itself will emerge from the inertia of a groundswell of like-minded people who are willing to act upon their dissatisfaction . . . The implication for us is that the second coming of the church will not be a clergy-driven reformation but a lay-driven explosion of spiritual angst and piety.

The most effective grassroots efforts are lean, streamlined coalitions. Adding more and more people is not the goal; the existing church has more than enough people to change the world. The new church must mobilize people with the appropriate perspective about the content of Christianity and its personal and cultural implications. When this happens, people will respond with an intense desire to be part of this transformational movement of God.

George Barna, The Second Coming of the Church

The "priesthood of the believer," the central goal of the Reformation, has been restored only theologically, not practically. It still exists mainly on paper. In very important ways, our churches remain closed to laymen.

James H. Rutz, The Open Church

This drawing of all members into the service, this mobility and unorganized unity, permitting variety which only emphasized the bond of a common life in Christ and indwelling of the same Holy Spirit, fitted the churches to survive persecution and to carry out their commission of bringing to the whole world the message of salvation.

E. H. Broadbent, The Pilgrim Church

3. Servant leadership

In Matthew 20:25,26, Jesus talks about leadership. He says, "You know that in this world, kings are tyrants, and officials lord it over the people beneath them. But among you it should be quite different. Whoever wants to be a leader among you must be your servant, and whoever wants to be first must become your slave." **There is no place in the body of Christ for the CEO model of leadership. Jesus modeled a servant style of leadership constantly.** He washed His disciples' feet. He did not expect to be served by them. Leadership should be from the bottom up. Look at this quote from a talk by Wolfgang Simson on the subject of apostles and prophets.

And what do I mean by apostles and prophets? Maybe with a few sentences I can explain what I do not mean. I do not mean powerful superstars; top-down guys who have it all and who answer the question, "Are you an apostle?" with the answer, "I have 150 churches working under me. I am supervising thousands. I am controlling and top-downing, drowning so many other churches." I'm not convinced that this is the way apostolic ministry works. I really am not.

I see Paul as a weeping father, crying his heart out for Timothy to overtake him, for Christ to take shape in the nations. I see him broken hearted—willing to let everybody walk over him. That's why in Ephesians 2:20, the Bible speaks about these ministries— the apostolic and prophetic—as foundations. Do like this with your feet, just for the fun of it. (Stomp, stomp.) Just hit the foundation of this house. Everybody needs it, but everybody tramples on it. It gives you a good idea about where apostolic and prophetic ministries belong. This is not a joke. Because in many ways this is exactly how they were treated and how they will be treated in the future.

The ministries and leadership in the house church movement seek constantly to ensure that every believer hears from God for him or herself. This does not mean that "every man does what is right in his own eyes" (Judges 17:6, 21:25) but that each believer has a truly sensitive spirit, and as such can discern the voice of the Lord.

Derek Brown

Once we understand that the purpose of authority is to release us to serve one another, we can begin to model the harmonious relationships we see within the Trinity. Such relationships need to be modeled within the church.

Martin Scott, *For Such a Time as This*

HOUSE CHURCH DNA

That's how you will find true apostolic people—usually you can diagnose them—they have a broken heart. They cry more than anybody else. In their wildest dreams, they don't think of building a big religious empire with themselves at the top and the others being grassroots. Would you like to be grassroots? Who wants to be grassroots? Don't raise your hand because grassroots sounds like doormat. It is a term invented by people who will explain laity in a new way too. I believe the apostolic ministries are mainly the weeping fathers. The meekness of their heart allows them to inherit the earth. Meekness you can't learn in seminary. Meekness you can only learn at the feet of Christ. Really you can only learn it there.

I believe that these people are very ordinary. They are approachable, no faces, no big names. Very un-intimidating. Let's say un-impressing. The thing that impresses me so much about Paul is that he is so unimpressive. He says that about himself. Weak, stumbling, stuttering—writes long letters. But a man you can easily reject. And I think, "Yeah—that is so different from the people who have it all together. Who are on the top because they deserve it so much! You know what I'm talking about. I'm talking about people who have somehow caught something of the heart of God that He's given them. I think that's normal. That's what He is doing around the world. To actually share His apostolic heart with apostolic people like John Knox. Good man, Presbyterian man. He was a Christian in Scotland. He prayed this prayer, "God, give me Scotland or I die." And God gave him Scotland. And then he died (Editor: John Knox was burnt at the stake).

Take women's ordination. *Christianity Today*–the fine, conservative, evangelical magazine published in the USA–interviewed me about the issue. "Are you concerned about the women the Church of England are about about to ordain?" they asked. "Not nearly as much as I am about most of the men they have ordained already!" I replied.

Gerald Coates, *Non-Religious Christianity*

If our understanding of authority is the ability to dictate to others what we wish them to do, we will always struggle. However, if we understand that authority is there to release those we are responsible for into their freedom, we will see how challenging and rewarding the exercise of true authority is.

Martin Scott, *For Such a Time as This*

Church leadership, as demonstrated in the New Testament, was always a plurality. There was no place for the one-man band. There is still no place for the one-man band. No one should be a law unto themselves, or beyond the authority of the team. New Testament leadership is "flat," or non-hierarchical. Of the fourteen times that the New Testament refers to a pastor or shepherd (Greek *poimen*), only one refers to a function in the church. The rest all refer to Jesus!

4.   Built on relationships

Church is family, and church in the home is modeled on healthy family life.

Even a casual read through the New Testament shows a depth of relationship between the believers that is rarely seen today. Jesus taught, "By this all will know that you are My disciples, if you have love for one another." The following comes from *Simply Church,* by Tony and Felicity Dale.

> *In the last part of Acts 2, and again in Acts 4, there is a graphic description of the way in which the early Christians lived. They shared their meals together, shared their possessions, and shared their lives.*
>
> *A very constructive exercise is to go through the New Testament looking for the "one another's." Amongst many other commands, we are told to lay down our lives for one another, to build one another up, to bear one another's burdens, to be kind and tender hearted toward each other, to admonish one another. These are not things that can be done while gazing at the back of someone's head in a Sunday meeting. They imply a vital sharing of our lives together, not just in meetings, but also day by day. Take the command to*

Except for cases in the New Testament where a church had just started, all the churches eventually had a plurality of eldership. In fact, there is no place in the New Testament where an established church is seen to have only one elder.

Bill Scheidler, *The New Testament Church and Its Ministries*

Even non-believers find the concept of community compelling:
"There is something magical about any intense, tightly-knit group of people working together and playing together, a feeling of being in the world while at the same time being apart from it, apart together. We believe that even those of us who have not experienced that magic hear its distant music, feel its ancient call."

George Leonard and Michael Murphy, *The Life We Are Given*

Jesus came to establish family, not a multinational corporation. His ministry was always geared to developing a grassroots outreach that operated in vivid contrast to that of the prevailing religious system. Jesus' focus was to blend present and future together into a startlingly new lifestyle. His doctrinal slant angered every religious group He encountered because it was so unique.

George Barna, *The Second Coming of the Church*

HOUSE CHURCH DNA

bear one another's burdens and so fulfill the law of Christ This means either that a person knows others in their church well enough to recognize when all is not well, or that a person feels safe enough to share the deepest things going on in their life when they are hurting.

The New Testament Christians obviously spent much of their time together. How can this be done in the busyness of American life today? Part of our problem is that we feel we can only invite others into our home if everything is perfect—not a speck of dust on the furniture, the kids all on their best behavior, and a cordon bleu, home-cooked meal sitting on the stove! If that is our standard, we will never get to know each other! Why not invite another family around for pizza before you take the kids to the ball game? Or invite a single parent and kids over just to share a movie? It will probably be the first invitation they have had for a while and might make your week!

When we lived in London, one of our home churches had several nurses in it, working really odd shift hours. We were in tough inner city London, and their only way home was to take public transport—not particularly pleasant late at night, to say nothing of the safety issues. That home church decided that they did not want those nurses using public transport late at night. So each week they would get the nurses' schedules and someone would meet them with a car whenever they came off duty to make sure they traveled home safely. That's fine for the first week or two, but think of the commitment involved when this goes on month after month! Now that is a practical expression of laying down your life for someone else!

Intimacy, sharing, community, and mutual ministry are better caught than taught. If the church planter modeled these traits, then they will be replicated throughout the churches as they multiply and divide.

Robert Lund, *The Way Church Ought To Be*

The house of God we belong to is one of relationships—relationships with the Lord and relationships with each other. What has been called a "loose association" is, in fact, a house of living stones.

Stan Firth, *Custom and Command*

HOUSE CHURCH DNA

We personally experienced this kind of commitment when we had really young kids. One of the single girls in the church decided that her ministry to Jesus was to clean our house each week. That was no small task in a hundred-year-old, four-story, London terraced home where there were three young kids and an endless stream of visitors. She would not accept a cent in payment! It is very humbling when others lay down their lives for you in such practical ways. It also builds deep friendships.

In the New Testament, the believers not only shared their time but also their possessions. None of them said that anything he had was his own, but they shared everything. Many years ago, we were challenged by A.W. Tozer's five vows, and one of those was that we were never to own anything. This means that the Lord can do what He wants with my possessions. If He asks me to give something away, it is not mine to hold on to. The principle here is stewardship rather than ownership. I need to take good care of the things that are entrusted to me. I may need to think twice before lending out my possessions to people who I know will not return them in as good or better shape than they received them. But apart from that, my material goods are not my own. Think how many resources could be released into the Kingdom if we shared, for example, our power tools, our lawn mowers, or our cars.

I will never forget another blessing that came our way. We were newly married and one of the people in the student church that we had helped to pioneer decided that we needed a car. Unbeknownst to us, she worked for the whole summer, and then presented us with her entire earnings. Imagine how

There is no virtue in just meeting in a home, but the meeting in a home is because of a fundamental belief that the people can only truly function in Relationship. The home is seen as a means whereby people can be "joined and knit together by what every joint supplies, according to the effective working by which every part does its share" which "causes growth of the body" (Eph. 4: 16). These relationships will be a true attempt to fulfill the commandment of Jesus to "love one another" (John 13:34) and will in themselves be a demonstration of true fellowship (1 John 1:7).

Derek Brown

surprised we were, how unworthy we felt, but also what an incredible blessing it was! And looking back on what that car enabled us to do as newly married students in a busy medical school context, I can see that we were able to touch many more people because of the travel time saved. She really had made her gift to Christ, and we were enabled by her generosity to live our lives more effectively for the Kingdom.

Sharing ourselves is often the most difficult thing to do. Paul could say in I Thessalonians 2:9, "We were willing to impart to you not only the gospel but also our own souls." In our culture it is not acceptable to show weakness. We all go around wearing masks. We wear the mask of a bright smile and "everything's fine," when actually our marriage is falling apart. Or maybe we don't know how we are going to put food on the table this week, or we are scared that our kids are going out of control, or we feel so depressed we don't know if we are going to make it through the day. The contrast to what has become the norm is illustrated by a passage such as I John 1:6 that tells us "to walk in the light as He is in the light and the blood of Jesus Christ will cleanse us from all sin." There is a transparency here, a willingness to let others see us as we truly are. Openness of this sort does make one liable to be hurt at times, but all loving relationships have the potential of causing hurt. Those we love the most have the most capacity to hurt us. Does this mean that I won't accept love because I refuse to risk hurt? Jesus loved us so much that He laid down His life for us. Love covers a multitude of sins. It also builds us up into a living demonstration of the body of Christ.

Do we feel safe sharing our innermost selves with a trusted brother or sister? It can take a lot of courage. Or from the other side, are we willing to respect confidences and to love unconditionally without judging? The book of I John is full of passages that talk about the need for us to love one another. Time and again it asks how you can love God, who you cannot see, if you do not love your brother. Our love for God is to be measured by our love for our brothers and sisters.

Are we prepared to rise up to the challenge of meeting the New Testament standard of building our church on relationships rather than just attending meetings or being part of the program? Are we willing to be inconvenienced in our personal lives to do this?

5. Simply Reproducible

There are a number of things that prevent a church from being quickly reproduced. As house churches, we have already dealt with the primary financial hurdles, in that we use homes or other centers of life rather than special buildings, and we would not normally expect or need paid leadership.

However, we do have other more subtle hindrances. For example, how often do we delay starting a church or "multiplying" one that is getting too big because we have no one to teach or lead, or no musician available. If we found a way of getting past these issues we could start churches more rapidly. In Acts 17, as far as one can tell, Paul was with the Thessalonians for three weeks before he was thrown out, and in Philippi, they were there "several days." So Paul must have faced these issues too.

Here in Austin we are simplifying our meetings so that even young believers can lead. We are basing our times together on

Simple is transferable, while complex breaks down . . . we must refine the process so that it is simple and transferable. Simplicity is the key to the fulfillment of the Great Commission in this generation. If the process is complex, it will break down early in the transference to the next generation of disciples. The more complex the process, the greater the giftedness needed to keep it going . . . The K.I.S.S. method works best for me. It stands for "Keep It Simple, Stupid!"

Neil Cole, *Cultivating a Life for God*

47

Acts 2 where "they devoted themselves to the apostles' teaching and fellowship, sharing in the Lord's Supper and in prayer." We come together for a simple potluck meal (which means no one has to go to a lot of effort, although it has led to some interesting menus!). We share what is going on in our lives. We read aloud a passage of Scripture, stopping for discussion whenever anyone has a question or comment. And we pray for one another.

"What! No worship?" Not in every group! Some churches will have musicians and so worship will flow naturally, while in others they may sing a cappella. Some churches may rarely have singing. Now, when we have our larger meetings, when the churches come together to celebrate, that is a different matter! However, in this way, the simpler meetings can be facilitated by anyone.

6.   Commitment to aggressive evangelism and growth

In this country, the house churches have a reputation, sadly well earned, of being insular and inward looking. We focus on certain aspects of the Christian life, emphasizing, for example, open meetings, or close fellowship—all good and necessary—while other things tend to get forgotten. Most of us are too comfortable in an environment where we know everyone. We don't like to think of disturbing the status quo. We pay lip service to the Great Commission and pray half-heartedly for the conversion of our neighbors. Most of us have no meaningful relationships with non-Christians.

After Stephen's death, Acts 8 tells us that a great persecution arose against the church and they were all scattered. Verse 4 states, "Therefore those who were scattered went everywhere preaching the Word." **If we want to be part of a rapidly growing, church-planting movement, then we need to be willing to have our lives affected and inconvenienced by a**

God has given us a plan for His church. It is found in the New Testament. It is a plan that is very simple, very natural, and very reproducible.

God's plan is so simple, that we often don't see it. I wonder if the devil has not blinded us from seeing it. It is a plan that will work under any circumstance: it will work in any culture; it will work in any geographical area; it will work in any political climate; it will work both in urban and rural areas; it will work under any economic condition; it will work anywhere!

Nate Krupp *God's Simple Plan for His Church*

Thus, St. Paul seems to have left his newly-founded churches with a simple system of Gospel teaching, two sacraments, a tradition of the main facts of the death and resurrection, and the Old Testament. There was apparently no form of service, except, of course, the form of the sacraments. Nor was there any form of prayer, unless indeed he taught the Lord's Prayer. To us, this seems remarkably little. We can hardly believe that a church could be founded on so slight a basis. And yet, it is possible that it was precisely the simplicity and brevity of the teaching which constituted its strength . . . By teaching the simplest elements in the simplest form to the many, and by giving them the means by which they could for themselves gain further knowledge, by leaving them to meditate upon these few fundamental truths, and to teach one another what they could discover, St. Paul ensured that his converts should really master the most important things.

Roland Allen, *Missionary Methods: St. Paul's or Ours?*

In its new iteration, the church must reinvent itself as a movement of believers zealously seeking to infect others with Christ's love and a passion to serve others. The second coming of the church will be less of a reinvention of Christianity than a return to authentic Christianity in its original form.

George Barna, *The Second Coming of the Church*

Practical Application:
List five relationships you have with those who do not know Christ.

If you do not have those relationships, are there things you can do or places you can "hang out" to seek to develop those relationships?

passion to see the lost find Christ. Without aggressive and purposeful evangelism, we are unlikely to see the magnitude of growth for which we long.

Leaders of church planting movements in other nations talk much about the need to saturate an area with the Gospel. That is fine in a country where there is little or no active witness for the Lord, but what does it mean in a country like the States where anyone can turn on their radio and hear a version of the Gospel, where books about Christianity are in the local supermarket, and wherever you live, there are several channels on television devoted solely to Christian programming. Non-Christians think they know about Jesus because they have watched church on TV. And they have often been totally turned off by what they have seen. The problem is that what they have seen may just be a parody or caricature of the real thing.

Serious thought needs to be put into this area and an alternative suggested. If we consider that the great majority of people who become lifetime followers of Jesus did so because they had a friendship with a Christian, perhaps our thinking should move in that direction.

7.   A commitment to the body of Christ

House churches have been around for a long time in this country. Sadly, they are frequently very critical of traditional churches and often are guilty of negativity towards the rest of the body of Christ. While we may not agree with or like some of what we perceive to be unscriptural practices and attitudes in the institution, **we dare not risk being a movement that is reactionary and founded on rebellion.** How can God bless such a thing? You've had problems with traditional churches in the past? Get over it! We should refuse to base our practices in simple churches on a reaction against the institution. Instead, let us bless our brothers and sisters in other, more traditional

There is a false dichotomy drawn between quality and speed. The frequent assumption is that faster implies weaker or inferior.

A friend from China

I have been a part of many groups that became very ingrown and boring largely due to not keeping one eye on the lost and afflicted around us. We ministered the gifts of the Holy Spirit to each other. On a number of occasions, I have observed miracles firsthand, but as we lost part of the focus of going to those who really needed Him most, we began to see His power wane in our midst. It is a danger for any group of Christians (large or small) to become so focused on our own problems that we forget the call to help others.

Robert Lund, *The Way Church Ought To Be*

It is rarely that we find anyone aglow with personal love for Christ. This love as a kind of moral fragrance is ever detected upon the garments of the saints. The list of fragrant saints is long. It includes men and women of every shade of theological thought within the bounds of the orthodox Christian faith. This radiant love for Christ is to my mind the true test of catholicity, the one sure proof of membership in the church universal.

A. W. Tozer, *That Incredible Christian*

Prayer Point:
What are we doing to encourage unity and appreciation for other Christian groups in our area?

structures. Let us honor and speak well of them, and seek to work with them wherever possible. This does not in any sense compromise those aspects of house church that we have come to appreciate and love. After all, Jesus did not pray passionately that we might agree with each other, just that we might be one! (John 17)

8.   Non-Religious Christianity

All too often, Christianity is seen as a religion of rules. Do's and don'ts (particularly the don'ts!) tend to govern our lives, and the joy of freedom and spontaneity flickers. In an effort to please God by "coming out from among them and being separate" or "loving not the world," we often live by the rulebook rather than trusting God that He has indeed transformed us from the inside out. **If we are genuinely a "new creation," we can live in the freedom of following the Spirit within us instead of trying to obey a set of external rules through our own efforts. When we were born again, God gave us a new heart with His laws written on it, not a set of commands that we have to strive to live by.** For the Christian who is seeking to follow God, doing right *is* what comes naturally! We Christians tend to live within a box of our own, often rigidly perceived views of what is or is not permissible to the serious disciple of Jesus. The church still tends to act like the Pharisees of old who "strain out a gnat and swallow a camel!" Christianity should be a lifestyle rather than a religion, a way to live life from the Source within, rather than a set of outward patterns of behavior that are somehow acceptable to the church.

One of the ignored names of Jesus is "Friend of Sinners." There are not too many choruses written on this theme! How many of us can say we have sinners as our friends? There was something about Jesus that was comfortable and not out of place at dinner parties with notorious sinners (Matt 9:10) where the

Many of the doctrinal divisions among the churches are the result of a blind and stubborn insistence that truth has but one wing. Truth has two wings.

A. W. Tozer, *That Incredible Christian*

Rainus Killus in Ecuador reports:

In December, 1984, two brothers from different churches approached me, asking me to join them for prayer every morning from 5am to 6am. Only a couple of weeks later, a number of other Christians joined us. We prayed specifically for unity and reconciliation between Christians. After two months, there were 20 of us.

Then they started to report that people were being saved in their churches without effort or evangelization. In our church, we repeatedly experienced healings: the lame walked, and people were freed from epilepsy and demonic bondage. During that time, I noticed that I had to "keep my arms up." If I prayed for less than one hour each day, the church started to stagnate, and if I prayed longer, the growth continued. In October 1990, I handed a church of 250 adults and 150 children on to my successor; one year later, it had grown to 800 people.

FridayFax

The God of the modern evangelical rarely astonishes anybody. He manages to stay pretty much within the constitution. Never breaks our bylaws. He's a very well-behaved God and very denominational and very much one of us, and we ask Him to help us when we're in trouble and look to Him to watch over us when we're asleep. The God of the modern evangelical isn't a God I could have much respect for. But when the Holy Ghost shows us God as He is we admire Him to the point of wonder and delight.

A. W. Tozer, *The Missing Jewel of the Evangelical Church*

wine flowed a little too freely (Matt 11:19), and even prostitutes might show up (Luke 7:36). Yet I would not be seen going into a bar (so as to avoid even the appearance of evil). Now obviously we are not talking about participating in sinful practices, or deliberately putting ourselves in sin's way, but rather a willingness to let go of our self-righteousness and hypocritical adherence to what others judge to be acceptable standards of behavior. And we are not talking about excuses for failing to follow God with our whole heart. But for the serious disciple, walking into a bar (unless he has had a problem with alcohol) does not constitute a sin. Nor does having a beer with friends. Getting drunk does! Walking into a bar and striking up a conversation with someone may save a soul from hell. Hanging around with non-Christians is not a sin. Enjoying their company is not a sin either! (A person can instinctively tell if we are only with them because we have another agenda, i.e., that of witnessing to them and then if they do not respond, losing interest in them.) A genuine friendship with someone who does not know the Lord is the most likely way, statistically, that they will come to follow your Best Friend too.

Our legalism only serves to confirm the view of a God with a big stick waiting to catch the unwary in some unsuspected sin. We have a church building near our house with a large sign in front that has a verse of the week displayed. Most of the time, these verses are harsh and condemning. Who would be interested in that kind of a God, especially if He only speaks in King James English? Too often the church's gospel is bad news! Jesus reserved His harshest criticisms for the legalists of His day. As the Word says, "the letter kills but the Spirit gives life."

The Gospel is Good News! Jesus was immensely attractive and winsome to the seeking unbeliever. People respond to love, not condemnation. Jesus did not condemn the woman taken in adultery, just encouraged her not to sin again. May our lives,

There is a major difference between behavior regulated by law and behavior regulated by grace. They may appear to be the same, but their motivation and source are completely different.

Gerald Coates, *Non-Religious Christianity*

We are not fulfilling a list of rules. When the Spirit of promise came, the promise was that you will not do these things. As we walk in faith, embracing the promise of God, conscious of His presence—we fulfill the promises.

Gerald Coates, *Non-Religious Christianity*

Somebody once remarked to another, "Won't it be good when we are all in heaven. The Roman Catholics will be able to eat meat on a Friday!" The listener responded, "Yes, it will also be a place where the Jews can eat pork chops all day long!" There was lots of laughter. The initiator of the conversation picked it up again: "Heaven will also be a place where evangelicals can drink in front of each other!" (more laughter!) There are all sorts of things that religion hinders people from doing openly. Secret drinking generally means there are other secret areas of our lives. It is the secret areas of our lives where Jesus is not Lord.

Gerald Coates, *Non-Religious Christianity*

Religious people perform superficially what only Christ can change fundamentally. Christianity has little to do with meeting the standards of superficial behavior. Religious people and religious churches cut themselves off from reality.

So you either live by rules and laws for yourself and for others, or you choose to live responsibly with your freedom. But the end result seems the same . . . If God looks upon the heart, however, He knows that much of what we do has nothing to do with our heart, loyalties and affections. It has to do with pleasing the crowd, or gratifying a demanding God.

Gerald Coates, *Non-Religious Christianity*

too, be attractive and winsome to the outsider because we genuinely love them. Lord, deliver us from being modern day Pharisees!

9.   Kingdom Lifestyle

Jesus taught more about the Kingdom of God than other subject. There are more parables on the Kingdom than any other topic. The disciples were instructed to announce that the Kingdom was near. If someone was healed they were to say "The Kingdom of God is near you now." Wherever He went, Jesus spoke about the Good News of the Kingdom. Between His resurrection and ascension, what He discussed with His disciples was the Kingdom. Yet we hear so little about it.

What is the Kingdom? Matthew 6:10, the Lord's Prayer, states, "Your Kingdom come, Your will be done on earth as it is in heaven." The Kingdom is where Jesus is King. It is where His will is being done here on earth. It is not just our Sunday mornings and Wednesday nights. The Kingdom is 24/7 living for Jesus.

Neither is the Kingdom limited to our times gathered together. If we are living for the Lord, the Kingdom is wherever we might happen to be, in whatever context. So for my husband, Tony, as a doctor in London, the Kingdom was in his medical office. If a patient presented with more than just a physical complaint, he would share with him about the Lord. If there were nothing that medicine could do to help them, he would pray for their physical healing or deliverance. Sometimes he had words of knowledge for these non-Christians. Often they were healed or set free, and the Kingdom had come near. And hundreds of them became Christians. There was one period of time when his regular nurse was on maternity leave and someone from our church with a real gift of evangelism took her place, and every day for six weeks, at least one person became

It is amazing, but perhaps not surprising, how people are willing to apply the law and Scripture to everybody else, but seem not to apply it to themselves. According to Jesus, that is Pharisaism.

Gerald Coates, *Non-Religious Christianity*

You can make more friends in two months by becoming interested in other people than you can in two years by trying to get other people interested in you.

Dale Carnegie, *How to Win Friends and Influence People*

Bart: "What religion are we?"
Homer: "You know, the religion with all the well-meaning rules that don't really work in real life!"

The Simpsons

It comes back to what we are focusing on. Christianity is a way of life. Christianity is living as Jesus would live if He were in your shoes, which in fact He is! Anything other than this is just a religious system—Churchianity! We find ourselves doing what keeps the church happy rather than what keeps Jesus happy.

Tony and Felicity Dale, *Simply Church*

The primary goal for the house church is the Kingdom. Any kingdoms that are built by man (including religious kingdoms) are seen as man-made structures that will inevitably be shaken. The Kingdom is seen as something that is received (Heb 12:28) and represents every aspect of life that comes under the rule of God. As the Kingdom affects every area of life, there is no sacred, secular or other divisions in life. All of life comes under the Lordship of Christ.

Derek Brown

a Christian. This is "Your Kingdom come, Your will be done" out in the market place.

What does it mean for most of us? For the businessman, it means using Kingdom principles of honesty and integrity in business. For the secretary, it means living as Jesus would in the office. For the student, it means seeking to put Him first at school. Every situation will be different, but "the kingdoms of this world are to become the kingdoms of our God and of His Christ" (Revelation 11:15). Sometimes it may mean that we risk our reputation. Often we have to step out of our comfort zone to follow where the Holy Spirit is leading. But as Jesus is lifted up, He will draw all men to Himself.

Kingdom living is living every moment of the day as Jesus would. As the saying goes, "He has no hands but our hands." Let's live in the light of "What Would Jesus Do?"

Kingdom removes the division between sacred and secular. It means there can no longer be one set of standards for when we are in church or with our Christian friends and another set for living the rest of life. The different compartments into which we divide our lives need to be integrated into one Kingdom-centered life.

Kingdom is living the reality of our Christian faith out in the marketplace where it can be seen. It is the church in the workplace, or in the home, at the ballpark, or running the P.T.A.. Living like Jesus means involvement in social action. "For I was hungry, and you gave me clothing. I was sick, and you cared for me. I was in prison, and you visited me."

Practical Application:
What are some ways in which you could bring the Kingdom into your daily life?

Practical Application:
1). Within the group studying this section on DNA, which of the 10 areas listed do you feel you are:

a) strongest in?

b) weakest in?

How can you work on the areas of weakness?

2). DNA is the basic building block of reproduction. What steps can your group be taking towards reproduction?

ven given am

on plan is for all, not jus

that everyone who believes in him may

not send the Son into the world to cond

through him." (John 3:16-17 NRSV) Ho

e willing to confess and turn from our ol

that teaches about Allah's love and forgiven

s, the Bible teaches that God's love and forg

but through Jesus' death on the cross. J

accept that atonement for the

Jesus allows us to h ve

Nothing turns off the next generation quicker than believers whose words don't match their experience. Children and new converts easily see where we deceive ourselves, just like the little boy in *The Emperor's New Clothes*. They will not tolerate form without substance, and many of them reject Christianity because they see nothing real about it.

Wayne Jacobsen, *The Naked Church*

Another aspect of the church's function is summed up in our Lord's oft-repeated phrase, "the kingdom of God." According to Jesus, the kingdom of God is equivalent to the reign of God. And God reigns in the hearts of men and women whenever they enthrone His Son, who is the King (Matt 25: 34; Luke 1:33; Rev 17:14; 19:16).

When Jesus was on earth, His ministry was chiefly centered on extending the reign of God. As He preached the gospel, healed the sick, cast out devils, raised the dead, fed the poor, reproved oppressors, and trained His disciples, He destroyed Satan's work on the one hand and extended His Father's kingdom on the other (Matt 4:23; 12:28-29; Acts 10:38; 1 John 3:8).

As the community of the King, the church exists to carry on the earthly ministry of Jesus (Matt 18: 19-20; Mark 16:15-20). As the corporate expression of the Risen Christ, the church is called to advance God's reign and destroy Satan's work in the earth (Matt 10:7-8; 16:17-20; Luke 10:18-20; John 14:12). As the recipient of the outpoured Spirit, the church is equipped to fulfill the mission of Christ, which is to "preach the gospel to the poor, heal the broken-hearted, preach deliverance to the captives, recover sight to the blind, set at liberty them that are bruised, and preach the acceptable year of the Lord" (Luke 4:18-21). In short, the kingdom of God is embodied in the person of Jesus, and the church is the instrument for its earthly expression.

Frank Viola, *Rethinking the Wineskin*

. . .Not only where the Lord Jesus is, but also where the church is, the kingdom of God is. Not only does the Lord Jesus Himself represent the kingdom of God, the church also represents the kingdom of God . . . The work of the church on earth is to bring in the kingdom of God. All the work of the church is governed by the principle of the kingdom of God.

Watchman Nee, *The Glorious Church*

THE GREAT OMISSION

In our western culture, speaking generally, the Great Commission has become the great omission. There are a few megachurches that see hundreds of people become Christians each year. According to David Barrett of the World Christian Encyclopedia, it costs $330,000 for each newly baptised person. Tragically, the "average" evangelical church only sees one or two new converts a year. Since we all know of churches that see hundreds converted each year, this means that, actually, the "average" evangelical church probably sees no converts in any given year! What has happened?

One of the features that characterize church planting movements in other nations is their commitment to aggressive evangelism. On a recent visit to India, for example, the zeal of five girls, between the ages of fifteen and nineteen, who spent their weekends out in the villages proclaiming the gospel, put us to shame. It did not matter to them that there was a high chance that they would get ridiculed or thrown out of the village. They burned with a passion to see souls saved and churches planted. In many countries of the world, people pay a high price to preach the gospel. They are beaten to the extent of having their limbs broken. They are thrown into prison—some may even lose their lives. Yet, they count it a privilege to suffer for the sake of the Gospel. How anemic our Christianity appears in comparison!

Hear the passion in the following passage taken from a talk by an Indian church planter:

> God asks Abraham, "Are you willing to go? If you are, we'll do business. If you don't go, the whole matter is finished." Jesus came to go: "This is why I have come, to go" (Luke 4:43). In Luke 13:33, "Today, tomorrow, the day after tomorrow I must go." That is what Jesus said and did. This is not once a month, or once every other month evangelism. If you want to be His disciple, it must

If you do for the next 10 years what you have been doing for the last 10 years, what difference will it make to your city, the nations?

Wolfgang Simson

Could a mariner sit idle if he heard the drowning cry?

Could a doctor sit in comfort and just let his patients die?

Could a fireman sit idle, let men burn and give no hand?

Can you sit at ease in Zion with the world around you damned?

Leonard Ravenhill

How shall I feel at the judgment, if multitudes of missed opportunities pass before me in full review, and all my excuses prove to be disguises of my cowardice and pride?

Dr. W. E. Sangster

be every day. So, the first condition is to go. If you are willing to go, God is willing to do business with you. If you are not willing to go, it is finished.

You will not go where you want to go; you will go where God goes. You will go where the cloud goes. You will not go as a Christian family and sit there and have some nice tea and crumpets. You will go, and God will take you. Our God is a going God.

In Matthew 28, the verses known as "the Great Commission" say, "All authority has been given to Me in heaven and on earth. Go therefore and make disciples of all the nations, baptizing them in the name of the Father and of the Son and of the Holy Spirit, teaching them to observe all things that I have commanded you; and lo, I am with you always, even to the end of the age"(NKJV).

One of the many lessons we learned in India this last visit is just how little of the Great Commission we in the West obey.

- The Great Commission says, "Go." Yet we ask people to come! Come to church; come to our special meeting. We need to be out in the marketplace, taking the Kingdom with us and starting churches where the people are.

- The Great Commission tells us to make disciples. But we seem satisfied to go and make *converts!* We are content with the sinner's prayer, when Jesus says that if the new convert loves Him, "[they] will keep My commandments." In Matthew 16, Jesus says, "I will build My church." We compound the problem by all of our efforts to build the church, rather than letting Jesus do it Himself.

- The Great Commission tells us to make disciples of nations. We are ecstatic if we see one individual come to Christ! We have little concept of bringing a nation to the Lord. I

Most churches today are trying to figure out how to get lost people to come to church. The key to starting churches that reproduce spontaneously is to bring the church to the lost people. We're not interested in starting a regional church, but rather to church a whole region.

Neil Cole and Paul Kaak, *Organic Church Planting*

The same is true of the "sinner's prayer." Many have gone through the ritual, thinking it a small price to pay to escape guilt or hell. In our haste to bring people into God's kingdom we too have lost true purpose to the outward form. We count converts by sinner's prayers or baptisms, never questioning whether or not these people are finding intimacy with God.

Wayne Jacobsen, *The Naked Church*

The significant problems we face cannot be solved at the same level of thinking we were at when we created them.

Albert Einstein

Practical Application:
Who are the unreached
people groups in your city?
Are there obvious ways to
reach them?

recently took a brief look at a list of the unreached people groups (Biblical "nations") of our city, and realized that only the middle-class, white families in our city were adequately evangelized. Those that had yet to be targeted in any meaningful fashion included:

- The youth
- University students
- Yuppies
- The elderly
- Blacks
- Hispanics
- The wealthy
- People who live in apartment complexes (50% of Austin lives in multi-housing units and 95% of them are unchurched!)
- Various other nationalities (Other than the Chinese, no other group appeared to have adequate numbers of churches.)
- The housing projects

If you ask an Indian church planter how he knows when a nation is considered to be discipled, he will tell you it is either when there are indigenous leaders who are raising other leaders from that people group, or when an indigenously led church planting movement is going on.

- We fail to teach them to obey all that Jesus has commanded. If you look at the statistics from someone like George Barna, the sociological indices of the church here in the USA are very similar to those of the world: a virtually identical divorce rate, the percentage of those abusing alcohol or drugs is similar, much the same numbers of Christians as non-Christians look at pornography, particularly on the Internet. The church has failed to teach its members to obey the commands of Jesus. "Well," you may say, "I hear sermons all the time on this kind of thing." Then there is something wrong with our teaching methods when they make so

"From a missionary perspective," I asked [Richard], "what makes a people group reached?" His reply verbalized a previously held, yet unspoken conviction of mine: "A people group is considered 'reached' when a church starts another church without the help of an outside group. Then we have a church planting movement . . . the goal of every missionary."

Joe Boyd, "Missionary Church Planting", *House2House Magazine*

Tell me, in the light of the cross, isn't it a scandal
that you and I live today as we do?

Alan Redpath

One can be a fully paid-up, tongues-speaking charismatic, meeting in a hired facility with a five-piece band and no hint of anything which is outwardly religious. But, if what happens on a Sunday morning when we break bread (or at any other time) doesn't affect how we treat one another for the rest of the day, we are into religion, not faith. If we can walk away from a meeting which is filled with the presence of God and manifestations of the Holy Spirit and gossip over lunch or watch a blood-letting violent film, blasphemous comedian or sexually explicit feature film without a tinge of conscience, we are into religion. If we can sing of God's grace with furrowed brow and mega sincere heart and mercilessly judge those who are different from us or who have hurt us, we are into religion.

Gerald Coates, *Non-Religious Christianity*

One of the greatest deceptions of Satan himself to the church, in order to disarm it or weaken it, is to lie to us that all what we need is more and more anointing. What good is the anointing if we cannot walk pure lives?

Chris Daza

little difference in the way people live out their lives!

- Once the disciples have been equipped, then they need to be released to go out and plant more churches, and so the whole cycle will repeat (John 20:21).

Obedience to the Great Commission will make the difference between whether our churches are just cozy huddles where existing Christians are seeking a personal blessing, or whether they become church planting movements that have the potential to profoundly affect this nation. Are we willing to be personally inconvenienced in order to obey Jesus' command? Do we dare risk getting out of our comfort zone in order to reap the harvest?

The fields are white and ready to harvest. Will we go?

Practical Application:
What do you see as hindrances for yourself in intentionally "going out into the harvest field"?

This is obviously a vast subject and there is no way that we can do it justice within the confines of a manual such as this! However, there are certain aspects that will be underlined, specifically as they relate to house church Christianity.

Intercession for the nation

Psalm 127:1 says, "Unless the Lord builds the house, those who build it labor in vain." There is a great need for intercessors to undergird and sustain what God is doing with the house churches in this country. I believe this move has been birthed in prayer, (e.g., by the current prayer movement), but if it is not nurtured on our knees, it could rapidly go off course or just fizzle into nothing. We need to spend much time on our faces before the Lord. We cannot expect a move of God cheaply— let's be a people who will pray the price.

In 1983, we had the privilege of visiting Full Gospel Central Church in Seoul, Korea. I remember thinking before we went that a church of that size (around 350,000 at that stage) had to be superficial. The night we arrived, the temperature was several degrees below freezing and since the room where we were staying was unheated, we decided to go early to the all-night prayer meeting in the hopes of getting warm. Arriving at least an hour before the scheduled time, we found the place (which seated 10,000) packed out – women with babies on their backs, children sleeping on the floor, old people, young people, all worshipping. We did not understand a word of what was going on, but when the meeting started, everyone began to pray in unison, loudly, crying and shouting out to God. They stood, hands raised, some with fists clenched, tears running down their cheeks. It was profoundly moving. After a while I looked at my watch. Forty minutes later, someone rang a bell and the praying stopped. Then another topic was announced and off they went again. And so it went on all night. I felt humbled, that I was only in kindergarten as far as prayer was concerned. And that was the pattern for the next few days. We met several people

Our praying, however, needs to be pressed and pursued
with an energy that never tires, a persistency which will not
be denied, and a courage which never fails.

E.M. Bounds

Whole days and weeks I have spent prostrate on
the ground in silent or vocal prayer.

George Whitfield

From the day of Pentecost, there has not been one great spiritual awakening
in any land which has not begun in a union of prayer, though only among
two or three; no such outward, upward movement has continued after such
prayer meetings declined.

Dr. A. T. Pierson

Revival is no more a miracle than a crop of wheat. Revival comes from
heaven when heroic souls enter the conflict determined to win or die—or
if need be, to win and die! "The kingdom of heaven suffereth violence,
and the violent take it by force."

Charles G. Finney

who had fasted for 40 days, and many who had seen amazing miracles in response to prayer. At the end of our time there I was convinced that we had been seeing a mighty and deep move of the Holy Spirit in response to the fervent prayers of His saints.

We have a need for intercessors who will storm heaven on behalf of what the Lord is doing with house churches in this nation, and do battle on their knees against the principalities and powers arrayed against us. My limited experience of fasting and intercession is that, although it might sound spiritually 'glamorous,' actually it is hard work. Frequently it seems as though the heavens are as brass, and my prayers get no higher than the ceiling! The fruit of these times, however, is more than I have even dared to imagine in terms of answered prayer and seeing God move in power.

Some years ago I was asked an interesting question. If I had to choose between a move of God typified by thousands being touched by the Holy Spirit, with manifestations of His presence such as people falling before the presence of God and other signs and wonders, and a slower steadier work with thousands coming into the Kingdom that transformed a society, which would I prefer? My answer had to be that I would prefer the latter, such as we had experienced on our visit to Korea. I recently read an interview with Dr. Cho in which he said that until the last few years, he had to pray for four to five hours a day to see God move in the kind of power that they were experiencing. Now he has been able to cut down to three! Intercession is a hidden work that involves many hours on one's face before the Lord. Are there people in this nation who will pay that kind of a price? Will I?

Prayer for laborers in the harvest

I find that there is one particular prayer that I am praying with increasing frequency and urgency. This is in response to Jesus'

Practical Application:
List five non-believers, whom you know personally, to pray for.

One quote that has helped me through the years is:

"Pray as if everything depended upon God;
Work as if everything depended upon man."

My wife and I are members of a church planting team here in Guayaquil, Ecuador. Prayer is our number one strategy for reaching the Guayaquil Mestizos, our assigned people group to Christ.

There is no doubt in my mind that everything depends on Him. He has moved to act through the prayers of His people. We have watched Him plant 89 house churches in the past 18 months and are acutely aware that nothing would have taken place apart from prayer and His working to build His church.

Our passion comes from wanting to collaborate with Him in what we see our Lord doing. We pray, watch, wait, and when we see Him moving, we do our best to get in line with His motions. An old German proverb says, "God gives the squirrel a nut, but does not crack it for him." God opens doors, but we have to walk through them.

Our short-term human goal is 100 house churches. I believe God's goal is that He wants "all men to be saved and to come to a knowledge of the truth . . . " If this is what Christ desires, then one million house churches is not out of line or egotistical. The question remains, are we willing to pay the price, in prayer and sacrifice, that one million new churches will require?

An interesting question for me is, what would have to happen in order for us to see one million new house churches?

Guy Muse

Alvin Vander Griend tells of an experiment done by a church in Phoenix, Arizona. Intercessors randomly selected 160 names from the local telephone book and divided the names into two equal groups. For ninety days they prayed for one group of eighty homes. The other eighty homes were not prayed for. After ninety days, they called all 160 homes, identified themselves and their church, and asked for permission to stop by and pray for the family and any needs they might be willing to share. Of the eighty homes for which they didn't pray, only one invited them to come in. Of the eighty homes for which they had prayed for three months, sixty-nine invited someone to come over; of the sixty-nine, forty-five invited them to come in.

Prayer makes a difference in the harvest because God's promise to answer prayer applies to our prayers for the lost.

Douglas A. Kamstra, *The Praying Church Idea Book*

command in Matthew 9:38 to "pray the Lord of the harvest to send out laborers into His harvest"(NKJV). For thousands of churches to be started, we need thousands of those who will be out in the harvest fields reaping. It is relatively easy to start a church. What we need is laborers who are willing to go out and do it!

Spiritual Warfare

I recently read a story about a soldier who, while sitting at a café waiting to go off to war, was picked off by a sniper's bullet. The fact that he had years of training and was fully equipped for battle made no difference. His problem was that he had not realized that he was already in the battle zone.

Ready or not, we are in a spiritual war. The world lies in the devil's hands and our mission is to claim back as much ground as we can. If we do not recognize the tactics of our enemy, we are liable to be rendered ineffective by one of his fiery darts.

Spiritual warfare is one of those areas that has gained a bad reputation recently because of the excesses and unbiblical practices of some of those involved. But this does not make the area any less of a reality. The answer does not lie in ignoring it, but in finding right and Biblical ways to wage our warfare.

Following Peter's great confession that "You are the Messiah, the Son of the living God," Jesus says, "You are Peter, and on this rock I will build my church and the gates of hell shall not prevail against it." What are these gates of hell that shall not prevail against the church? In New Testament days, a wall surrounded every city, and the one who had control of the gate had control of the city. So what are those things that control our cities? In some cultures these things are obvious; there will be temples or mosques, witch doctors or magicians. Here in the West, it is more subtle. Yes, there are fortunes tellers and adult video stores, but these do not abound on every corner. Here, the problems may be such things as materialism, intellectual-

We are not imaginary soldiers fighting an imaginary battle. Everything is real.

Chris Daza

We need to recognize that spiritual warfare has to do with our entire life-style. It is a battle process and not a scheduled function. It has to do with our spiritual welfare. Put it in another way, it has to do with the way we are faring in our spiritual life. In this regard, Spiritual Warfare is really Spiritual Welfare.

Chris Daza

If we understand that the enemy of our souls is out there on a daily basis, seeking someone that he may devour, then we will understand that the evil day talked about in this text lives with us 24/7... If Satan has nothing to accuse us of, because we are walking in truthfulness, righteousness, faith, in the word, in a salvation process, and clad with the preparation of the shoes of the gospel, how can the enemy stand against us?... Is it not clear that our greatest tool is what Jesus said in John 14:30, "the prince of this world is coming and he has no hold on me." Right there is the key, HE HAS NOTH-ING (NO HOLD) IN ME. If the devil has no hold on you, then you have authority over him. And that is what prayer really is, exercising authority over his hosts of demons so that God's kingdom would come. Our real authority is when Satan cannot accuse us of anything.

Chris Daza

ism, and Internet pornography, or in other areas, poverty and violence, drugs and immorality. These things control our cities. Yet, Jesus says that they cannot prevail against an attack by the church.

In Matthew chapter 12, Jesus gives an illustration in his defense against an attack by the Pharisees. They accused Him of casting out demons by the power of the devil. He replied, "How can anyone enter the strong man's house and carry off his property unless he first binds the strong man? And then he will plunder his house."

First, we need to identify the strong man. Then we need to bind him and finally we can plunder his goods. What are the strong man's goods? They are the people who are in his possession. So before we start a house church in a particular neighborhood we would do well to identify and bind the strong man that controls that area.

We saw this happen in a very specific way in one of our churches in a low-income housing project. The areas under the control of the enemy there were pretty obvious when we started—violence, drugs, immorality, etc.—and we did some specific praying about them. Not only have we seen many find the Lord, on a recent visit there we were told by some of the residents how much less fighting there has been there recently, and that some of the drug dealers have moved out! We still have a long way to go, but the changes are very encouraging.

Practical Application:
What strongholds does Satan have in your neighborhood?

God delights to answer specific prayers. If we just pray, "Lord save our city," God asks, "What do you want me to do?" If we come in a general way against the enemy, it is like dropping a bomb on an enemy country without having a definite target in mind. We need to pray specific prayers and to target definite areas of enemy activity. Then we will start to see answers!

So let's look at how we might spiritually prepare to plant a church in a neighborhood. Our aim (just like in war) is to have

It is a fact of history and experience that no army ever won a war on the defensive.

In the early part of this century, someone asked a well-known French general, "In a war, which army wins?" The general replied, "The one which advances."

…Many people have interpreted these words of Jesus incorrectly. They have somehow assumed that Jesus pictured the church on the defensive, being besieged in a city by Satan's forces. They have taken His promise to mean that Satan would not be able to batter the gate of that city down before Jesus came and caught the church away. That is really a totally defensive concept of the church in the world but it us completely incorrect.

…Jesus pictures the church on the offensive, attacking the gates of Satan. Jesus promises that Satan's gates will not hold out against the church and that Satan will not be able to keep the church out. It is not the church trying to keep Satan out; it is Satan failing to keep the church out. Jesus promises us that, if we obey Him as our commander-in-chief, we will be able to move out, storm Satan's citadels, break through his gates, release his captives, and carry away his spoil. That is the church's assignment, and it is essentially offensive, not defensive.

Derek Prince, *Spiritual Warfare*

It is against these [forces of darkness] that we wrestle and who does not know that wrestling is a very close contest. It is an intensive and difficult conflict that tests strength and strains every fiber of our being. It is a hand-to-hand, foot-to-foot. The king of this kingdom of darkness is a very experienced warrior who has fought many battles; he is not a coward and he is no casual adversary.

Chris Daza

the aerial battle won before we go in with the ground troops. What are the steps we could take?

1. **Do a survey of the land**. When Moses sent the spies into the land of Canaan, he was effectively doing a spiritual survey of the land before they went in. (Numbers 13:1-25) Joshua provides another example. When he was parceling out the land of Israel to the different tribes, he had men go out and survey the unconquered land and present a written report of their findings. (Joshua 18:1-7) In any modern warfare, the satellite and spy plane surveillance has already given our forces a very good idea of what they may face on the ground before any kind of strategy is developed. We should not be ignorant of the land that we are going to possess. We should walk the area, taking note of anything of spiritual significance and asking the Lord for wisdom concerning the spiritual powers that have dominance in that place. Then we will know how to pray.

2. **Ask the Lord for direction**. We should not immediately go into battle, but ask our General, the Lord, for wisdom. He will tell us what to do. Plan a strategy. Set up a group of people to pray for the area.

3. **Establish a prayer team**. Finding a team of people who will cover the whole project in prayer while others actually prayer walk is a vital part of the warfare against the forces of darkness.

We had a very interesting experience while we were in India that reinforces this point. We were at a church-planting seminar, and one of the speakers had given a message on spiritual warfare and prayer walking. Early the next morning, many had gone out and spent time prayer walking, particularly coming in prayer against the demonic forces behind various idols and temples. Later, during a teaching session, when people were giving a report back on what had gone on as they prayed, there

By the time Alexander the Great was eighteen, he was conquering most of the known world. His soldiers were eager to experience battle and prove their devotion and bravery to their leader in combat. Only then could they cut the letter "A" for Alexander into their body; it was a mark they were proud to display.

The comparison of a soldier is not inappropriate for the believer either.

"Endure suffering along with me, as a good soldier of Christ Jesus. And as Christ's soldier, do not let yourself become tied up in the affairs of this life, for then you cannot satisfy the one who has enlisted you in His army" (2 Timothy 2:3-4).

A soldier knows that he or she is never to underestimate the capability of his enemy; to do so is to invite defeat, and death.

The tactic of our enemy is not so much to steal you from God's salvation (which I believe to be impregnable Matt. 16:18), but to so distract us into focusing on the theology of God rather than God Himself, or so weigh us down with the circumstances and cares of this life that we become an ineffective element for the Kingdom of God.

The witness of His presence becomes missing in our life; that fragrance of Christ that was so evident at salvation disappears.

Years ago, I read an article in a magazine that is now out of circulation. In this particular article, a question was asked of a pastor from Africa.

"Why is it that we hear so often of miracles and signs and wonders taking place in Africa, yet here in America it is so few and far between?"

I could almost hear his deep Nairobian accent as he answered, "In America, you study God; in Africa, we worship Him!"

We have lost our lust, our desire, and our passion for the real presence of the Holy One in our fellowship, and have been satisfied for the "status quo" of churchianity.

It shouldn't be our "programs" or even our "great fellowship" or "fantastic teaching" that draw and keep people in church; these things soon wane. It should simply be His presence.

Jeffrey Collins

It is a basic assumption of military strategy that if you hope to win, your troops must:

Be aware that a battle is coming,
Be psychologically and emotionally prepared to fight the battle, and
Be equipped with the resources to fight effectively.

George Barna, *The Second Coming of the Church*

was a sudden commotion. People started scurrying around and eventually we discovered that a fire was raging out of control in the kitchen. A propane tank had been leaking gas, and an intense fire started the moment someone had tried to light the stove. Immediately people began praying. We went to look, and flames were licking the ceiling and bursting out the door of the kitchen. We estimate that the fire burned for at least twenty minutes before the local fire truck managed to put it out using a full tank of water.

It would have been so easy for the gas tank to explode or for someone to be burned. What was even more amazing, though, was that when we went into the kitchen after the fire was extinguished, there was absolutely no damage! There was not even smoke damage. Some glass jars were on a shelf immediately above the stove, and even though flames had been roaring around them, they were not cracked. The kitchen looked just as it had before the fire!

When we discussed it later, the impression everyone had was that the prayer walking and spiritual warfare had stirred up the enemy, and so he had tried to retaliate by causing the fire. However, the prayers of the saints had prevented him from causing any harm.

In some places, people have tried prayer walking and the attack against them has been so fierce that they stopped. The answer is not to give up, but to get adequate cover while we pray!

4. **Physically walk the area**. The book of Joshua tells us "He will give us everywhere that the sole of our foot treads." There is something very strategic about actually setting foot on the area we are seeking to reclaim for the Lord. When we prayer walk, there are a number of things we can do.

   - Lift up our eyes and praise God. Thank Him for His creation. Bless the city, especially that area and the people who live there. Bless the political leaders, the media, the

We have not yet resisted unto blood in prayer. We don't "even get a sweat on our souls," as Luther put it. We pray with a "take-it-or-leave-it" attitude; we pray chance prayers; we offer that which costs us nothing! We don't even have a "strong desire." Instead, we are fitful, moody and spasmodic.

The only power that God yields to is that of prayer. We will write about the power of prayer, yet we don't take it with us into the fight. As a church, it seems our title is "We Wrestle Not!" We will display our gifts, natural or spiritual; we will air our views, political or spiritual; we will preach a sermon or write a book to correct a brother in doctrine. But who will storm hell's stronghold? Who will say "No!" to the devil? Who will deny himself good food or good company or good rest that hell may gaze upon him wrestling, embarrassing demons, liberating captives, depopulating hell, and leaving, in answer to his travail, a stream of blood-washed souls.

Leonard Ravenhill, *Why Revival Tarries*

Should all the hosts of death
And powers of hell unknown
Put their most dreadful forms
Of rage or malice on,
I shall be safe; for Christ displays
Superior power and guardian grace.

Isaac Watts

"Christ in you, the hope of glory." I'm not afraid of the devil. The devil can handle me—he's got judo I never heard of. But he can't handle the One to whom I'm joined; he can't handle the One to whom I'm united; he can't handle the One whose nature dwells in my nature.

A. W. Tozer, *God's Greatest Gift to Man*

Solvitur ambulando. It is solved by walking.

St. Augustine

schools, the hospitals etc. Proverbs 11:11 tells us that the upright bless the city. We bless and do not curse the city, because it already lies under a curse from the enemy.

- Pray for the welfare of the people who live there. In Jeremiah 29:7, the people of Israel were told to pray for the peace and prosperity of Babylon, even though it was the land where they were held in captivity.

- Demolish the strongholds that are there. In the name of Jesus, bind the demonic powers that control the area. There is no need to become fanciful or strange in praying into these areas. Some people will want to imagine demons behind every tree. We are to use spiritual weapons to fight the principalities and powers. Jesus tells us that we overcome Satan by the blood of the Lamb and by the word of our testimony, and we do not love our lives to the death. In Matthew chapter 4 we see Jesus defeating Satan using the Word of God. Psalm 149 shows us that praise is another effective way of defeating Satan. Use the name of Jesus. The word of God is very clear that we can defeat the enemy. We have the authority to bind all the power of the evil one. (See appendix 2)

- Repent for the problems in the area. The problems of the city (corruption, drug trafficking, prostitution, business failures, etc.) are because the saints of God have not done their job in praying for the city and the redemption of those living there. I Peter 2:6 says that we are a royal priesthood. What was the job of the priest? Jesus as our great high priest gives us the example. He is making intercession for us at the right hand of God. One of our functions should be to intercede, to stand in the gap and plead for the lost. We sit in church while the rest of the world goes to hell because we enjoy our sleep or watching television too much!

The church, by virtue of her faithful use of prayer, wields the balance of power not only in world affairs, but also in the salvation of individual souls. Without violating the free moral responsibility of any individual, the church, by means of persistent, believing intercession, may so release the Spirit of God upon a soul that he will find it easier to yield to the Spirit's tender wooing and be saved than to continue his rebellion.

God will not go over the church's head to do things in spite of her because this would abort His plan to bring her to full stature as co-sovereign with the Son. He will therefore do nothing without her. To this John Wesley agrees when he says, "God does nothing but in answer to prayer."

In order to enable the church to overcome Satan, God entered the stream of human history in the Incarnation. As unfallen Man, He overcame and destroyed Satan both legally and dynamically. All that Christ did in redemption, He did for the benefit of the church, He is "head over all things to the church" (Eph. 1:22). His victory over Satan is accredited to the church. Although Christ's triumph over Satan is full and complete, God permits him to carry on guerrilla warfare. God could put Satan completely away, but He has chosen to use him to give the church "on-the-job" training in overcoming. Prayer is not begging God to do something which He is loath to do. It is not overcoming reluctance in God. It is enforcing Christ's victory over Satan. It is implementing upon earth Heaven's decisions concerning the affairs of men. Calvary legally destroyed Satan, and canceled all of his claims. God placed the enforcement of Calvary's victory in the hands of the church (Matt. 18:18 and Luke 10:17-19). He has given to her "power of attorney." She is His "deputy." But His delegated authority is wholly inoperative apart from the prayers of a believing church. Therefore, prayer is where the action is.

Paul Billheimer, *Destined for the Throne*

PRAYER AND PRAYER WALKING

We will not win our nation by doing social work or holding great outreaches or preaching great sermons. Psalm 2 tells us, "Only ask, and I will give you the nations as your inheritance, the ends of the earth as your possession"(verse 8). The battle for our nation will be won on our knees. The battle for our cities will be won in the prayer closet. The battle for our neighborhoods will be won as we wage spiritual warfare on behalf of the people living there. And once the strong man is defeated then we can plunder his goods and see hundreds and thousands set free from the kingdom of darkness and brought into God's Kingdom of light.

Prayer was an integral part of the early church meetings. It was not an option for a few members in the church who felt called to pray; rather it was a priority, ranking high on their agenda as they met. As for the apostles (the sent ones, the church planters, the pioneers, the missionaries), they soon realized that if the Commission was to be fulfilled, they were courting failure if they omitted prayer. They remembered that the way of their resurrected Master was the way of prayer. They had often seen him disappear into the mountains to have communion with the Father. They witnessed how He vanished from an ongoing successful healing and deliverance rally, away to lonely mountains, to be in the presence of His Father. They saw His success in ministry, that He was always at prayer, waging warfare with the archenemy and his hosts of darkness.

The apostles realized immediately that the only way to guarantee the same results that they had seen with Jesus was the way of their Master, by prayer and preaching the Word. Through this ministry, the sick were healed, the demonized set free, the dead raised to life. The book of Acts of the Apostles, (really Acts of the Holy Spirit,) recorded some of the result of all their prayers. They lived to see the day that the Lord had promised, "the works that I do you shall do also and even greater works than this shall you do". They had found the formula. It was not some methodology or model. It was the prayer life-style that He lived before them. Many times He left abandoned the many demands, requests and invitations, only to go to some lonely mountain to seek the will of His Father and fellowship with Him. It is this continuous fellowship with the Father that was really the source of His strength, radiance and success.

Chris Daza

STARTING A CHURCH

There are many different ways to start a church. The following are some ideas for starting a church using examples from our experience.

1. We had a number of business associates who were not Christian, but whom we had come to know pretty well over a period of months or years. We asked a dozen of them to join us in a study of business principles while enjoying pizza in our home, using the book of Proverbs as our textbook. There were no rules to our discussion; everybody's opinion was valid and there was no such thing as a wrong answer. Gradually we introduced prayer and worship and over the course of a year, every one of them became a Christian. They formed the nucleus of our original house church.

   Suggestion: Draw together people from your circle of influence.

2. When we finally decided that it was okay to start a church, we asked our kids to invite all their friends from our neighborhood to come for a breakfast Bible club. We picked a Sunday morning to do this, since we reckoned that all the Christian kids would be in church. We wanted to reach the non-Christians. The main attraction was a huge cooked breakfast. Before long, we had about 20 kids coming to our home. The majority of them became Christians and some started bringing their parents with them.

   We have followed a similar pattern recently with a group of older teens and twenties. Now we have a separate church that a number of their parents are coming to as well.

   Suggestion: Do something with your kids and their friends, and then include their parents.

3. A couple in one of our churches invited a number of families who live in their neighborhood to come and join them for church in their home. Because of the friendships that had been developed over some time, a number of people came.

How they met defined the Christian faith: the only templeless, clergyless and ritualless religion in human history! What a glory to the Carpenter and His faith!

Rugged, poor, tired people were the clergy, the living room their temple, worn out clothes their costumes. And Jesus Christ was the vocabulary.

Mark this. Mark it well: the church of Jesus Christ was born in informality. It ought to have stayed that way. It must be informal if it is to be captivating and meaningful to us. And to unbelievers who wander in! If our meetings are to communicate to the world what the *ecclesia* is and what the Christian faith is . . . then those meetings must return to informality. Our faith was born that way!

Gene Edwards, *How to Meet*

Not many were Christian at first, but they stayed because of the warmth of the fellowship and the sense of belonging.

Suggestion: Invite your friends and neighbors.

4. I approached a local assisted–living retirement center and asked if they would like to have someone hold a Bible study for their residents. (The term 'church' may be too threatening here.) They jumped at the idea, advertised it for us, prepared the room and have been very encouraging. The residents love it too. An 85 year old from another retirement center in the area now runs that group.

Suggestion: Do something with the elderly or where residents are living in an institutional setting.

5. One of our guys asked permission to use a room at work for prayer and Bible study. Shortly before 9/11 he was given a room. On September 11th the room was filled with people wanting to pray. There are now two groups meeting there and another at a different company.

Suggestion: Start church at work.

6. A couple came for just a couple of weeks before sensing that they could start something in their home and with their contacts. They had around ten non-Christian adults and a dozen kids at their first gathering!

Suggestion: Do not automatically assimilate new people into an existing group. This may be an opportunity to start in a new neighborhood.

Practical Application:
What are the obvious ways that you could start a church?

7. A family who are committed members of a major liturgical denomination felt they needed to reach out to others who were wanting to see their faith come alive. They meet mid-week for their "real church" while continuing to support their local congregation on a Sunday.

Suggestion: Start a church alongside a mainstream congregation.

P.O.U.C.H. churches

PARTICIPATIVE discussion characterizes Bible teaching. It centers on application.

OBEDIENCE to Scripture by members and the group is the measure of success.

UNPAID, often semi-literate lay-people co-lead.

CELL groups or small independent churches of about fifteen members are usual.

HOUSES are typical meeting places.

A friend from China

STARTING A CHURCH

Practical Application:
This chapter began with seven examples of starting churches, each followed by a suggestion.

Which of the suggestions might enable you to start a church?

When are you going to begin?

- Church planting is not the role of a special person. Everyone in the church needs to know that they too could start a church. All can be asking the Lord for an opportunity to do so. This is an essential part of the DNA of house church.

- In all of these examples, we are working primarily with non-Christians or the unchurched. There are plenty of people out there who are looking for something like this without needing to persuade our friends who are happy in their more traditional churches to come and join us. We are not into sheep stealing!

- It does not matter where the group meets, as long as it is somewhere people spend their lives. It is better, except when you come together for a celebration, to have many smaller groups (the sort of size that will fit into the average living room) than to keep getting larger. We will discuss how to multiply groups later.

- Some people will be gifted to start churches. There is no reason why a person should not be involved in more than one church plant at a time. They will probably move on to start other churches, leaving that one in capable hands. Last year I asked God if I could be involved helping to start ten churches that year. I asked and God did it!

Now we come to perhaps the most exciting principle in church planting and that is the concept described in Luke 10:1-10. This is the passage where Jesus sends out the 70 disciples in pairs to the villages where He was planning to go. We can have confidence that if Jesus instructs us to go to a place, then He will show up there too! We see this pattern of team evangelism and church planting continuing throughout the New Testament. In India, they are using this method to great effect. The following is taken from a talk given in India by a man who has been used to start over 3000 churches, mostly since 1997 (name withheld for security reasons). It obviously needs adapting to a Western culture. Street preaching in villages is not our normal approach. However, there are some dynamic principles here. It will take a major paradigm shift in our thinking on church planting, but we are seeing similar results where we have tried it.

Your mission is to harvest a field that is ready. When you go to a village to plant churches, you should understand that your business is to harvest all the people there, all the different castes and people groups. Your problem is that you have no laborers. Therefore, you are going there, not to preach and make a noise. You are going there to prepare laborers. This needs a change of mind-set, because most people when they go, they say, "We want to preach in that village. We have our drums, we have our bongos, we have our singing team and we have our microphone so we are going to preach." That is not your real purpose. Your real purpose is to prepare laborers there. That village is the field and that is where you are going to prepare laborers. You are not going to import laborers from outside because those laborers will go back. You might bring some laborers with you to train those people and then they will go back. Local laborers will take over. Your purpose in going there is not to preach, not to teach, but your real purpose is to prepare laborers, so when you leave that village, there will be some laborers still functioning there. Otherwise the field will be left without laborers and the harvest will not be protected.

In our mindset we go to preach, but Jesus is saying, 'No, you go there and prepare laborers.'

Then Jesus tells you what you have to take with you. Do you need to take bongos, drums, musical team, truck, and loudspeaker system? He says, "Please don't take anything with you." Don't take extra clothes because you don't have to stay there. You think, "I will stay here forever!" Don't do that! That is the implication of taking nothing with you. You go there, take care of your business and come back.

Try and compare what we do with what Jesus is recommending. Let's look at Jesus' method versus our traditional methods.

In verses 5 and 6, Jesus is defining how you are going to do it. He says when you go, go very quietly. Don't even greet anybody. When we go, we go singing loud and clear – bang, bang, bang. Everybody needs to know we are going to preach. Jesus said, 'No, don't even greet anybody. Go very quietly. Today we are beginning to understand why He said that. Five or ten years ago we could go to a village like that, making a noise. We can't do that anymore because a reception party is waiting for us. We might not come back safely. We might come back with broken legs. So He says to go very quietly. Don't wake up the sleeping devil. Let him sleep there. You quietly go and prepare your laborers and then come back and the laborers will take over there.

There is one more very significant reason. When you go on a mission like this, you are also praying as you go. Obviously you are praying because your objective is to take possession of that village. You are going to establish a house church, and through that you take possession of the village. So you are praying, "Lord, give me this village," because God said, "Ask me and I will give you the nations for your inheritance." So you are asking for that village, maybe you are even doing spiritual warfare as you go because you know there are temples there, mosques there, and idols there. There are all kinds of

Everybody has a ministry in Nepal nowadays. I was in one of their big conferences where there were over 2000 representatives. I asked them, "All who have been persecuted, please raise your hands or stand up," and almost half the people stood up because they were being persecuted. This was not mild persecution. There were people who had broken bones or serious injuries, and there were those who went to prison for over a year. That country has paid the price. They didn't become Christians just because there are good evangelists. They are willing to undergo persecution for their faith. That is the kind of Christians we are to produce, those who are willing to stand for their faith and to fulfill it.

Indian Church Planter

witch doctors there. One of the reasons why you should be going quietly is because you are entering into enemy territory. At the moment that village is in the possession of the devil. He has full control of that village and you are entering into enemy territory to take that village away from him, so you are praying on your way, quietly.

The first thing you need to do is to find a man of peace. You greet the house and if the Son of Peace is there, then your greeting will be accepted. If not, it will come back to you. So basically you are looking for a man of peace. Your purpose when you go to a village is not to preach. Jesus is defining that you first look for a house of peace, because that is where you are going to plant your church. This man of peace is a very important concept. In the Greek, the word is 'huios eirene'. Huios means son, eirene means peace. He is not a Christian. He is a peaceful man; he might be Muslim, or anything. He is a man of peace; he is not at war with people, or with himself. He is also an influential man. And how do we know he is the man? Because he will say, "Please come and stay with us."

This man will invite you into his house and will say to you, "Please come and have a cup of tea." You tell him you have come to talk about the Kingdom, and he says, "Oh, yes, please tell us about the Kingdom," and then after some time he says, "Why don't you stay and have lunch with us?" and he tells his wife, "Please make lunch." So it develops from one step to another and you know this is the house of peace, this is the man of peace. He is the laborer who you will develop as the leader, and he will know the strategic people too. You don't go from house to house. But if he says, "We have to go to that house because someone is sick there," you go. You are appointing a person who is going to take authority in that village. Jesus says "You go and stay there," and then he says, "You eat."

But when do I start preaching? You know, we brought this team and we brought many people and I am ready to preach now, so

Jesus in Luke 10:1-9 instructs the 70 as they go into the towns to look for a "man of peace." This man is already prepared to receive the good news of God's Kingdom. He has a good reputation and has good relationships with many others in the community. This man's home becomes the center of activity for the evangelist, from which the message penetrates the whole community.

Dick Scoggins, *Planting House Churches in Networks*

The person of peace principle is clearly illustrated in the book of Acts. Cornelius was a God-fearer, a Jewish proselyte, who was well-known for his generosity to the Jewish people. He demonstrated the person of peace principle by inviting Peter and his companions into his home. We see a similar situation with Lydia in Acts 16. Nothing in her story implies that Lydia was seeking the God of Israel. But clearly she had a hunger for God. On hearing Paul, she opened up her home. This is characteristic of the person of peace.

Tony Dale

when do I start preaching? This is where Jesus says "No, no, no, don't preach, please, just wait."

In verse 7 Jesus says to eat and drink whatever is laid before you. It is important to eat whatever is laid before you. You don't say, "Sorry, I don't eat pork. I only eat chicken." In verse 8, Jesus reminds us again that whatever house you go into, please eat. Two verses consecutively. This has a very important connotation in our culture, because within the caste system in our villages, people cannot eat with each other. So when we eat together it means we have a relationship. Jesus is saying that until this relationship is created, you cannot preach. The gospel will not take root. And if you don't eat - maybe you are with a low caste family and you see some flies on the food, and it doesn't look so nice and it is dirty and you say, 'No, I don't want anything to eat,' - that person will be offended. Eating produces relationship. Relationship is what people are looking for. If you don't have relationship, you can give a wonderful sermon but nothing happens. There is no fruit to be seen.

So when you go to a village, your first business, Jesus says, is eat, even if there are flies – eat the flies and all. Don't say no. Whatever is laid before you, you eat it as it comes. This is Jesus' style. This is preaching. Creating a relationship is a lifestyle preaching. You are teaching a lifestyle. Think of examples where Jesus ate with people; Zaccheus, Matthew, Martha and Mary, the Pharisee. In Zaccheus' house, Jesus did not preach. He just ate and everything happened. Zaccheus preached, and all the notorious sinners who were there were converted. This was not by Jesus' preaching but by Jesus eating with them and showing His humanity in fellowship with them. Much of Jesus' ministry revolved around what is called table fellowship.

Then, Jesus says, after you have eaten, you still don't preach, still no meeting. He doesn't believe in meetings. The word 'meeting,' as we use it, doesn't come in the Bible anywhere. In verse 9 it says 'then you do signs and wonders.' So you

The biggest movement in India is based on eating and drinking. It is a very low caste group and their leader has some workers who he has trained. Nearly 100,000 people have been baptized. So I asked him, "How did you do it?" He said, "It's very simple. You just follow Luke 10 and you will get conversions." I asked him, "What do you do in the village?" He said, "I go to the village and then I will sit in the shade just outside a family's house and I ask the lady of the house, 'Can you give me a glass of water?' She looks me up and down. I am so well dressed that she thinks I am from a high caste, so she doesn't give me water. Meanwhile, I am talking to the men. After some time I remind her, 'I asked you for water, but you didn't give me any. Is there a problem?' Again, she doesn't know what to do with this fellow because she thinks he is from a high caste, in which case he will not drink the water. She thinks the whole thing will be an embarrassment because maybe he doesn't know that she is low caste. Then again, a third time I will ask, 'I asked you to give me water. What is the problem? You are not giving me water.' Then she will go and whisper something to her husband asking, 'What shall I do?' Her husband will usually come to me and say, 'Excuse me, do you know what caste we are?' I say,'I am from the same caste as you, so where is the problem? Why don't you give me water?' They say, 'You don't look like you're from our caste.' That is when I preach. I say, 'If you believe in Jesus Christ, you will look like me.' They begin to ask, 'Who is Jesus Christ?' He tells them about Jesus Christ and he says he not only gets water, he also gets dinner and by next day they are all baptized. So there are baptisms every day. I think last month they baptized 8,000 – on an average they baptize 8,000 per month – all based on relationship, eating food, drinking water.

Indian Church Planter

pray for these people. You cast out demons. If people have problems, you lay your hands on them and you pray for them. When Philip, the first evangelist, went to Samaria, most of his ministry was about healing the sick, casting out evil spirits and so on. That is preaching. He is the evangelist. So signs and wonders, healings and deliverance and solving of problems, these are your preaching. Once healings happen and deliverance takes place, the fear of the Lord comes. People ask, 'How did this happen? We went to that temple, we went to that witch doctor, we offered coconuts, we offered gourds, we offered chickens, we spent so much money, went to so many doctors, nothing happened. These people come, they are here for five minutes, they pray and the person is healed.' So they are awestruck. Now they will ask you, 'What is this power? We went to all the others and nothing happened. What is this power that you just speak a word and in two minutes the evil spirit is gone. This person is healed.' Now when they ask you, 'What is this power?' then you tell about Jesus. And a house church is established because they are asking the questions. This is your preaching.

In this way a church is planted. Now they will ask you, 'When are you coming back again because there are a lot of other people who need prayer?' Now is your chance to say, 'Yes, I will come back, but you saw what we did. You can do the same. When we are not there and sick people come, you pray in the name of Jesus, and if you have faith they will be healed. All you need is faith.' So you are leaving a laborer behind. You are not leaving a vacuum. If they say, 'No, no, we can't do it,' say, 'Okay, we will come back and teach more until you are able to do it.' After two, three or four visits you will find that person will say, 'Brother, you were not here last time and a woman came, who was so sick she had not eaten for many days and she couldn't get up, and I didn't know what to do because I couldn't contact you, so I prayed. You won't believe it. It was so exciting. You won't believe it, this woman got up.' So their faith is increased.

Revival in the Himalayas

A few years ago in the Christmastime snow, Caleb (name changed) wanted to go shopping. He was new in the Himalayas and wanted to stop in a town before traveling on. He noticed a group of passers-by gathered around a girl who was obviously demon-possessed, screaming and breaking the chains with which people had tried to keep it under control. A witch doctor was trying to drive the spirits out, but with no apparent success. Caleb was unsure of himself, so he walked past to carry on with his shopping. "But within me, I was sure that Jesus could help the girl, so I eventually went back and offered to pray for her," he says. "The witch doctor simply smiled, and showed me the long list of sacrifices which he claimed the girl's family would have to make in order to appease the gods, telling me that I obviously did not realize the power of the spirits here. I remained steadfast, and was finally allowed to pray in Jesus' name. In my uncertainty, I prayed in tongues for the girl, and within a few moments, she calmed down and was completely freed. That caused some excitement, and the bystanders started asking where I lived and who I was."

"At 5 a.m. the next morning, we were all awoken by loud knocking: some 70 locals stood in front of the house, torches in hand, asking if Jesus lived here. Somewhat cautiously, we answered that he did, because he lives in us. At first we thought that the girl had relapsed, and the people had come to kill us. That was not the case! They had brought a number of sick people, and wanted us to pray for them before we moved on. It was amazing: every time I laid hands on someone, I knew exactly what to pray, and every person for whom we prayed was healed or set free. A steady stream of locals prevented us from continuing our journey that day as planned; we prayed with them until 8 p.m. There must have been 3,000 in total. We told them about Jesus as well as we could, and remained in the town. In a short time, so many people came to faith in Jesus that we could hardly keep count of how many we baptized. We began to organize them into house churches; the movement has become so strong that I estimate that already 10% of the population in the region follow Jesus," Caleb told us recently. "I sometimes wonder what would have happened if I had simply ignored Jesus' voice telling me to pray for the girl on the street that day."

Name withheld for security reasons

LUKE 10

Basically you are planting a house church in that house, the house of peace, and it is a permanent thing. This is Jesus' method of church planting – very simple, very inexpensive, very effective. And it multiplies because once the man of peace has taken charge, every time you go, teach him something more. Then the whole family gets baptized. So the whole household will come into the Kingdom. And so it is so much easier for you, so much easier for them and so much easier for the community there because this influential family has now come into the Kingdom.

Let me illustrate how these Luke 10 principles are working here in the States.

Around eighteen months ago, the Lord showed us prophetically that we were to start a church in one of the low-income housing projects about twenty minutes from our home. So we gathered together a team to pray for the area, and for several months, it was a prayer project. From time to time we would actually go and walk the area claiming it for the Kingdom, but most of our praying was done on an individual basis.

One day, Tony and I happened to be driving by, and on impulse, decided to stop and prayer walk again. Tony was specifically asking the Lord that we would meet our 'person of peace.' A torrential downpour surprised us and we ran to take shelter under a balcony with two Hispanic ladies who turned out to be sisters. Conversation started, and they inquired what we were doing there. (We obviously did not fit the local profile!) We explained to them that we were praying for their neighborhood, and as the conversation went on, asked if we could come by occasionally to pray about the needs in their family. They immediately agreed, and so for the next few weeks, once or twice a week we would drop in and pray for them, staying just fifteen minutes or so. It was not long before we were seeing very specific answers to prayer.

LUKE 10

One of the sisters, Lily, turned out to be our person of peace. (She has a heart as big as Texas—everyone is welcomed and loved by her.) Our next step was to ask if she would bring some of her friends and family members together, and so a weekly meeting time was set up at her home. She very quickly became a Christian, and this led to many of her family members also doing the same. We have touched several other homes in the complex, too. Now a year later, her apartment is crowded out every week with 30 to 40 people jammed in, sitting on the stairs, on the floor, kids everywhere. Neighbors are telling us that the project has begun to change; there is less violence and some of the drug dealers are moving out. We have started a church in the home of another family member in a different housing project as well.

Another interesting side benefit is the effect recently it has been having on some non-Christian teenagers, friends of our own kids, who go along with us to help with the younger ones there. They are being profoundly touched and moved by what they are seeing there, and for some of them, it has been a large part of their own journey towards salvation.

The 'person of peace' is such a key concept for us to understand. These are the laborers whom God is going to use to bring in the harvest. In the examples given in the last section, most of the people involved are 'men of peace.' The problem is not that the harvest is not ready. The harvest is ripe. Lord, send forth laborers into the harvest!

Practical Application:
How could I locate and identify a person of peace in my neighborhood, or in my work place?

SUGGESTED STEPS FOR PLANTING A HOUSE CHURCH IN YOUR NEIGHBORHOOD

1. "Prayer saturate" the neighborhood (II Chron. 7:14; Jer. 29:7),

2. Look for a "House of Peace" to be revealed (Luke 12:5-6).

3. Convert it into "A House of Prayer for all nations" (Mark 11:17).

4. Disciple the seekers.

5. Baptize those who repent and accept Jesus as Lord (Matt. 28:19).

6. Equip them for ministries for the edification or growth of the local body of Christ (Eph: 4: 12). Preferably equip them on site.

7. Send them out to repeat the whole process, "As the Father has sent Me, so I send you" (John 20:21).

   Results:

   Rapid multiplication of quality churches: "And the churches were strengthened in faith and grew in numbers daily" (Acts 16:5). This should result in mushrooming numbers of churches in farms, factories, offices, worksites, teashops, market places, schools, colleges and, of course, homes.

   Transformation of communities, cities, and nations (II Chron. 7:14).

8. Take this on war footing—until the knowledge of the glory of the Lord fills the sea. Then Jesus will come as King of kings and Lord of lords, and we will rule with Him forever (Hab. 2:14 ; Rev. 1: 5-6).

You are commanded to love your neighbor as yourself. The best thing you can do is to pray him or her into the Kingdom (Luke 10: 27, 37).

Amen. Even so, come Lord Jesus.

Indian Church Planters

EQUIPPING THE SAINTS

Jesus never commanded us to plant churches. He told us to make disciples and said that He would build His church. II Timothy 2:2 encourages us to "teach these truths to trustworthy people who are able to pass them on to others." Hebrews 5: 12 says that those who have been Christians for a while ought to be teaching others.

Jesus, in the Great Commission, told us to teach the new disciple to obey all the things that He had commanded. Discipleship is learning how to live a life of obedience that will equip for a lifetime rather than a body of knowledge to be learned. By making discipleship into a series of doctrines or teachings, we are robbing the new believer. Discipleship is equipping to live rather than educating through a series of doctrines. It is answering questions on real life issues and dealing with the things that are of relevance to that person. It is a process of learning to live as a follower of Jesus.

Throughout the New Testament it is obvious that new disciples were equipped for life in the Kingdom. What was taught? How were they trained?

Here are some of the areas in which they were equipped:

Entering the Kingdom

- Salvation and the Lordship of Christ.
- Baptisms – in water and the Holy Spirit.

Living in the Kingdom

- Praying in faith
- Studying the Word, and then obeying it
- Hearing God
- Finances
- Relationships
- Spiritual gifts, especially prophecy
- Church life

Village people don't come to the Lord because we give a good sermon. They come because we disciple them, and discipling means solving their doubts, problems, and questions. It is entirely questions and answers, highly interactive.

Indian Church Planter

Discipleship in Jesus' day was casting out demons, healing the sick, identifying with the powerless, laying one's life down for one's friends and even those who are not of the household of faith. How different today. Discipleship is going to university, then Bible college and getting into a form of ministry where one's contact with the unbelieving world is minimal.

Gerald Coates, *Non-Religious Christianity*

Discipleship for Jesus was relational. He called His disciples to be with Him (Mark 3:14). He lived with them, ate with them, rejoiced with them, and wept with them. Over and over His love for them is stated and displayed. They were not students of a class He taught, nor were they "ministry projects" upon which He worked. They were brothers whom He loved and to whom He was dedicated. He lived with them, worked with them and loved them in such a way that their lives were changed forever. Such is the ministry of discipleship.

Dick Scoggins, *Planting House Churches in Networks*

Advancing the Kingdom

- The nature of spiritual warfare—how to overcome Satan.
- Setting others free—evangelism, deliverance, healing etc.
- Starting churches

(See Hebrews 6:1-3, Matthew 5-7, Mark 11:20-26, II Corinthians 10:3-6, I Corinthians 11-14, Luke 4:18-19 etc.)

How were they taught?

The disciples of Jesus were taught not just in teaching sessions (which appeared to be very interactive with discussion and questions and answers), but also, as Jesus lived out His life with them, they had a vibrant daily experience of the outworking of His teaching.

People need to be trained and equipped in practical ways for life in the Kingdom. The idea of an apprenticeship is very appropriate here. Head knowledge is of little value; everything needs to be down to earth and relevant to life. For example, if we were trying to teach new believers about prophecy, the principles would be discussed, demonstrated, and then practiced until they were comfortable hearing the voice of God and then giving a word of prophecy. The more quickly a person moves into ministry, the faster they will grow.

It is also very important that the new believer learn to pass on what they are learning to others. In parts of China, they use discipleship chains.

> One way to ensure participation and maturity of development of each believer is to utilize discipleship chains. A discipleship chain relationship is one that takes place outside of the regular church meeting. It is usually a one-on-two discipleship process…The pattern is that a more mature believer disciples two others from within the congregation, each of whom disciples two othesr, who

We may see a wide variety of so-called Christians, but the Bible recognizes only one kind—disciples. Disciples are those people whose hearts burn with an unquenchable hunger for God, desiring to know Him better every day. They are not perfect, but they love Him and continue to draw near Him to learn how to trust Him more and be changed into His likeness.

Wayne Jacobsen, *The Naked Church*

Learning is not only hearing, but seeing how it is done, then doing it, and finally teaching it yourself to others.

Wolfgang Simson, *Houses That Change the World*

Everything we do, as individuals and as a group of believers, must be at His command: doing His will—totally, completely, fully, carefully, instantly, joyfully!

Nate Krupp, *God's Simple Plan for His Church*

In some ways its speed of development and high expectation and demands of new believers in the discipleship chain is what makes it more effective. Speed is not necessarily inversely proportional to quality.

A friend from China

then disciple two others. Each discipling relationship involves mutual accountability for putting into practice scriptural truth that is learned and teaching what one has learned. This twofold accountability is extremely important. (Editor's note: They take this very seriously. If the person being discipled has not put whatever the subject of the previous session was into practice and taught it to at least two others, they will cover the subject again until that has happened)

In order for this process to work, a person need be only one step ahead of the person whom he or she is discipling...

As a rule the discipleship chain...will not exceed four generations, plus the unbelievers that the last generation is "teaching."

A friend from China

We have also come across a very simple method of accountability groups that we are using with great effectiveness with some of our young Christians. Produced by Church Multiplication Associates (phone: 562-961-1962, www.CMAresources.org), it is a grassroots tool to help people grow in their spiritual lives and empower them to reproduce disciples. It combines three key elements:

1. Having accountability relationships

2. Reading scripture

3. Praying for friends who are not yet Christians

Discipling provides the building blocks of reproducing churches. Jesus commanded His apostles to "go and make disciples of all the nations, baptizing them in the name of the Father and the Son and Holy Spirit, teaching them to observe all that I commanded you." Their implementation of the plan is recorded in the book of Acts. And what was this implementation? The apostles went and planted churches. These churches, in turn, reproduced disciples who in turn went out and planted new churches.

Dick Scoggins, *Planting House Churches in Networks*

WHEN YOU COME TOGETHER

What should we do when we get together? One of the important things to realize is that church as a small group is not like anything else you may have experienced as "church." We get asked, "Is it like a prayer meeting?" We pray, but no, it is not like a prayer meeting. "Is it a Bible study?" No, it is not like a Bible study, although we will usually spend some time over the Word. Perhaps the greatest temptation we have is to make it a mini version of a larger meeting, where someone has been delegated to prepare some worship songs, another has a teaching, etc. If we do that, we have not gained much from meeting in a smaller group. Small group dynamics are totally different from those of a larger group.

Church is family. A normal family, gathered around the dinner table, does not have, for example, the mother say to the children, "Now let's all listen to what Dad has to say," and then the father talks for 40 minutes explaining something that is not of much relevance to the kids. No. Normal family is interactive, participatory and intensely relevant to the people there. And church should be the same way.

The Holy Spirit needs to be the One who controls the agenda in our times together. He has the plan for what needs to be accomplished. If we will learn to hear and follow His promptings, we will never have a boring meeting!

I Corinthians 11-14 talks about what we should do when we come together. Chapter 12 spends much time explaining how vital every part of the body is, and how each part has a different function. This needs to be expressed in our times together. I Corinthians 14:26 is the key verse for our meetings. It says that when we come together, each one has a contribution to make. Whether a song, a teaching, a revelation, a tongue or an interpretation—everything must build up and edify the body.

According to Acts 2:42 when the believers came together, they "devoted themselves to the apostle's teaching and fellowship,

In the NT, one gets the impression that a meeting of brethren ought to be more like a football team huddle, hospital, family mealtime, spontaneous party and military troop rally—these being daily events rather than once a week. These similes paint a picture that is a far cry different from what most Christians' church life is like.

Robert Lund, *The Way Church Ought To Be*

This everyone-involved type of gathering happens very naturally when believers gather in homes and sit in the normal seating of the home. Please don't drag in a pulpit and put the chairs in rows!

Sometimes the everyone-participating, normal gathering of the church is altered a bit if a traveling apostle, prophet, or teacher comes through your area and meets with you. Then the everyone-participate gathering allows room for the brother or sister to share, as took place in Acts 20:7-11. Room was made in the gathering for Paul to share. But he did not "take over" or monopolize. In fact, the Greek word, as we have already seen, means "converse, discourse, argue, discuss, dialogue." He dialogued with them. He talked—but they also participated.

Nate Krupp, *God's Simple Plan for His Church*

The Holy Spirit, for some reason, did not give us blow-by-blow descriptions of day-to-day body life and church meetings. Otherwise, we would have mimicked and worshiped the outward forms of the church, instead of continually seeking the mind of Christ for the near infinite number of ways that the principles and patterns which reflect the NT wineskin could be expressed. Indeed, much of Christendom has been slavish adherence to heartless rituals. We are to honor and implement the apostolic traditions that Paul spoke of, being careful to maintain underlying NT values, while avoiding the mere mimicking of outward ritual.

Robert Lund, *The Way Church Ought To Be*

the breaking of bread and prayers." These are the four elements that we try to include in the times that we spend together.

The Apostles' Teaching – Study of the Word

If our house churches are going to multiply rapidly, we will no longer have the luxury of taking several years to train a Bible teacher. Often, a new Christian will be leading something after only a short period. Paul faced this too—in some instances he moved on very quickly. For example, in Philippi he only "stayed for several days"(Acts 16:13). Therefore, we need to use an approach that allows the Bible to teach itself, where even the youngest Christian is able to lead.

We evangelical Christians tend to emphasize the importance of good *teaching*. This is missing the point. The essential is that people are genuinely *learning and applying* Scripture to their everyday lives. Statistics show that we learn far more by actively participating than by hearing alone. Scientists tell us that we remember 20% of what we hear, 50% of what we see and hear and 70% of what we hear and see and then say ourselves. In house church, we have the opportunity to involve everyone. In New Testament times, teaching was far more interactive; for instance, the word used for Paul's lengthy teaching in Ephesus is the word 'dialegomai' from which we get our word 'dialog' (Acts 20:7). Jesus tells us that we are to teach new disciples to obey His commands. In a small group, there can be some kind of accountability built in. More than once, we have had people say to us that they learned more in just months of home church, than they had in years of sitting listening to good sermons!

We try to spend little, if any, time in teaching in a formal fashion, but rather elect to have interactive discussion of a Bible passage. Over the years, we have come back repeatedly to three different methods of Bible study that are discussed below. The method is not important, but the fact that the method leads

There is a different way to meet for every race, every nation, every culture and every tongue. Each culture meets in a way distinct from the others. How to meet is a way to be found, not imposed. It is an adventure on a sea few have dared to sail.

Gene Edwards, *How to Meet*

In a small group that interacts like a family, everybody is talking, everybody is sharing, everybody is learning, everybody is maturing. Everybody in their testimony and witness is becoming more and more effective, because their questions and problems have been dealt with. Then they go back into their community, and can disciple other people very quickly.

Indian Church Planter

Though it was a century before comparable movements emerged in England, early Baptist meetings there possessed a similar character. Except where they were forced by persecution to gather in fields, lanes, and even caves, they initially met in private dwellings, barns, or rented rooms. A letter dating from 1608 describes a typical meeting. It included general prayer among those present, reading of Scripture and conversation about its meaning, extemporaneous teaching as several members were led by the Spirit, a concluding prayer and exhortation by the main speaker of the day, and a collection for the poor. There was also opportunity for members to engage in loving actions toward one another. The average length of such smaller meetings was around four hours. Once a month, several groups would come together in a combined gathering for corporate worship and mutual accountability, as well as to organize gifts for the needy in the wider community.

Robert and Julia Banks, *The Church Comes Home*

to a participatory discussion is important. Each of the three requires a facilitator. Their responsibility is to make sure the study keeps moving, that everyone is taking part and that no one person (particularly the facilitator!) dominates. It is not the facilitator's job to answer questions that come up. Rather he should direct questions back to the group, "What does anyone else think?"

In this type of Bible study, everyone's opinions are valued and there is no such thing as a wrong answer. But what if someone starts teaching heresy? (Christians always seem worried by this possibility!) In dozens of these groups over the years, we have never seen one sidetracked by wrong teaching. The Bible, rather than the leader of the group, becomes the authority. Even with the youngest Christians someone always says, "That doesn't seem right," if anything too outlandish comes up. A good facilitator will require some kind of Scriptural backing for any opinion voiced.

Usually our churches study their way through a book. Sometimes as much as a whole chapter will be covered in a session; more frequently, just a few verses. Because literacy may be a problem in some groups, we usually read only a couple of verses before stopping to discuss what we are learning.

Method I

A couple of verses are read, and then the group answers three questions:

What does it say?
What does it mean?
What difference does it make in my life?

You may wonder if there is any difference between questions one and two. But take the phrase from John 1 where it says, "In the beginning was the Word." There is a huge amount of meaning in there that could get missed if the second question were

Practical Application:
Get together a group of friends and try out the different methods of Bible study. I suggest using passages such as;

Acts 2:41-47;
Acts 13:1-4;
I Corinthians 9:19-23;
I Corinthians 14:26-40.

(You'll be surprised how much you learn!)

The meeting of the church envisioned in Scripture was designed to allow every member of the assembly to participate in the building up of the body as a whole (Eph 4:16). Mutuality was the hallmark of the New Testament meeting—"every one of you" was its most outstanding characteristic. While praise and worship songs were sung, they were not confined to the leadership of a special group of "professional" musicians. Rather, the meeting was open to allow for "everyone" to minister through singing . . . In such an open context, it is reasonable to assume that the early Christians regularly composed their own songs and shared them with the rest of the saints during the meeting.

Each believer who possessed a word from God was given the liberty to supply it through his or her own particular spiritual gift. Hence, a typical New Testament church meeting may have looked like this: a child shares God's word through a drama presentation and a song, a young woman gives her testimony, a young brother shares an exhortation followed by a group discussion, an older brother expounds a portion of Scripture and follows it up with a prayer, an older sister tells a story out of her own spiritual experience, several teenagers discuss their week at school and request prayer, and the whole group experiences table fellowship during a shared meal.

Frank Viola, *Rethinking the Wineskin*

I'm sorry to burst your bubble here, but every major heresy that has inflicted God's people in the last 2,000 years has come from organized groups with "leaders" who thought they knew God's mind better than anyone around them.

Wayne Jacobsen, *Why I Don't Go To Church Anymore*

not included. We use this method in our churches that meet in retirement homes. It is very simple and easy.

Method II

This is a modified Navigators' method. A couple of verses are read, and we look for things that correspond to three different symbols. The first is a question mark, which obviously symbolizes something a person does not understand. The second symbol is a candlestick and is used to represent something that sheds light, either on another passage of Scripture, or else something that is going on in a person's life. The third symbol is an arrow, and stands for where God is piercing a person's heart – they know that they have heard from God and need to do something about it. So a person might say, "I have a candlestick on this verse. This describes a situation that happened to me at work last week…"

We used this method to start our present group of churches. We pulled together a dozen non-Christian business people and studied the book of Proverbs looking at principles relating to business and wealth. Over the course of the study, every person became a Christian!

Method III

The third method we learned from Robert Fitts.

> *In discussion Bible Study we simply read the Scripture, each taking turns reading a few verses, depending on how many people are present. While it is being read, everyone is invited to interrupt at any time and make a comment or ask a question."*

> *Alpha Omega Bible College*

If it seems that too much is being read, then the facilitator will stop the person reading and ask, "Does anyone have a comment?" It is unusual for more than a few verses to be read

In fact, we have discovered that the younger the adult, the less interested he or she is in a smooth presentation. Excellence and professionalism are "performance strategies" that appeal to the late Builders and early Boomers. Among the Busters, however, the keys are relevance, genuineness, and authenticity. They are more interested in experiencing a sincere and honest presentation that raises meaningful questions, than a polished, well-rehearsed speech that provides all the answers.

George Barna, *The Second Coming of the Church*

Increasingly we find that young people view sermons as lectures, or class presentations, that are ineffective, one-sided communiqués. Churches that have experimented with interactive learning times, dialogical sermons, and other forms of Socratic communication are hitting a resonant chord among younger adults. To the Buster mind, participation in the process of learning and arriving at truths or principles is even more crucial than the truths themselves.

George Barna, *The Second Coming of the Church*

This may be a surprise to some, but there is no place for "preaching" in the gathering of the saints. There are five Greek words that have all been translated into the English word "preach" and all similarly mean "herald, publish, announce, proclaim, tell" the Good News. All of the instances where these Greek words are found in the New Testament are in the context of announcing the Good News to the lost and are not found in the setting of the believers' gathering.

Preaching is to take place out where the lost are: door-to-door, the streets, the market place, the fields, the highways and by-ways.

Nate Krupp, *God's Simple Plan for His Church*

before a discussion develops.

Our churches that meet in the housing projects use this kind of study.

The method used is not important. It is just a tool to accomplish the goal of a participatory Bible study. Here the Bible itself is the teacher, and everyone in the group is involved in both the teaching and learning process and the application of what is learned to daily life.

Are we saying there is no place for traditional teaching? Our experience is that the small meetings in homes are not the best place for extended, lesson-type messages. If God has revealed some helpful or exciting truth, do share it—in a brief form. But the cold fact is that listening to long discourses does not turn people into teachers!

Our larger meetings, where several house churches come together, have two main differences from the smaller meetings: First, the chances of getting to say something are definitely smaller. Over time, everyone can speak, but not in every large meeting. Second, the larger numbers often justify inviting in a gifted believer who has a powerful message or anointing.

Fellowship
Studies of early church history show that it was as much the love that Christians had for each other, as the actual message itself, that won so many to their cause. That this love went across culture, religion, ethnic differences and even the slave/ free barrier was a great testimony to all.

Just a casual reading of the New Testament forces one to the conclusion that the early disciples shared their lives together in a deep and meaningful way. In this country, and at this period in time, fellowship has tended to be superficial at best, and at

Wesley encouraged his people to stay within their local Anglican churches, but it was the smaller, class meetings within the larger Methodist societies that constituted the heart of the movement.

The primary point of belonging was that this more intimate level of community and membership in a class was required before one could join the society. The class meeting was the cornerstone of the whole edifice. The classes were in effect house churches (not classes for instruction, as the term "class" might suggest), meeting in the various neighborhoods where people lived. They normally met one evening each week for an hour or so. Each person reported on his or her spiritual progress, or on particular needs or problems, and received the support and prayers of the others. Advice or reproof was given as need required, quarrels were made up, misunderstandings removed. And, after an hour or two spent in this labor of love, they concluded with prayer and thanksgiving.

Quote from J. Wesley, taken from *The Radical Wesley: Patterns of Church Renewal* by H. Snyder

times downright absent! How can we change this?

Jesus taught that the world would know we are Christians by our love for one another. The apostle John, described as "the disciple whom Jesus loved," shared deeply on the nature of fellowship in his first letter. "If we walk in the light, as He is in the light, then we have fellowship with each other…" An old song we used to sing in England went like this:

> *Let us open up ourselves to one another,*
> *Without fear of being hurt or turned away,*
> *For we need to confess our weaknesses*
> *To be covered by our brothers' love,*
> *To be real and learn our true identity.*

True fellowship is like this. It is being real with one another, loving and caring for one another, genuinely and without hypocrisy. It is knowing if someone is having difficulties because we are familiar with them enough to recognize the signs. It is being willing to let down the masks that we all put up ("Yes, I'm fine, thanks," with a bright smile when inside we are barely under control) and risking letting people know us as we really are. True fellowship takes time and commitment.

John's conclusion in his letter: It is hard to believe that you love God who you cannot see, if this is not being matched by love for your brothers and sister who you can see.

Breaking of bread

We have been involved in home style meetings now for most of the last 30 years, and we have come to the conclusion that there is one factor more important than any other in determining whether a group will be successful or not. Do they share meals when they get together? Those that eat together invariably do better than those that do not.

Eating obviously played an important part in early church life, as it did in Jesus' life. Some of Jesus' most effective times

When you walk into that first-century ecclesia, what you see are people who know one another, who are daily spending their lives together, helping each other in every way they possibly can. They are in one another's lives . . . These people, with all their problems in interpersonal relationships, are at the same time loving one another . . . If you do not have that element, in abundance, visibly overwhelming you, you simply do not have the ecclesia, no matter what you think you may have.

Gene Edwards, *How to Meet*

Biblical fellowship involves people sharing together the reality of their spiritual journey. They trade insights into His ways and seek counsel in difficult circumstances, encouraging each other to greater trust in Father's working. They serve each other even when it is inconvenient, are honest with each other even when it is difficult, and pull together instead of pulling each other apart. Even if it's only two or three others, find some believers with whom you can meet regularly. Worship together, share your study in His Word, and support each other through prayer and practical service.

Wayne Jacobsen, *The Naked Church*

And when they meet *all* of them carry the meeting. All the body, caring for all its parts. They are in love with *Him* and with His beautiful fiancée. In a word: They are the embodied, visible, living, breathing body of Christ.

Gene Edwards, *How to Meet*

Practical Application:
In our small group, are we always expecting the same person to provide most of the food?

with unbelievers included food, e.g. Zaccheus, Matthew's friends, etc. Many of the occasions described with His disciples involved a meal, e.g. the Last Supper, and His times with the disciples after His resurrection. Acts 2:46 reveals that the early church shared their meals daily with great joy. 1 Corinthians 11 tells of the problems that arose when some people failed to share the common meal, during which they remembered the Lord's death in the communion, appropriately.

Eating food together does something to the way that people relate with each other. We have found that it produces an informal atmosphere that makes it much easier for people to share their lives together. However there are some guidelines that we use. As in everything else, we try to make it easy to duplicate. If a host family produces a gourmet meal, that makes it very intimidating for others who think they have to live up to that standard. In general, we have a simple potluck meal together. Everybody brings a contribution. If it is in the evening, we may have those who work just bring something that they can pick up at a store, such as sodas or a dessert. Occasionally there are drawbacks to not organizing it more, such as the time when every single family brought some kind of pasta dish. But in general this approach works very well. We try to make sure that people help with the clean up, and if we know there are families who are struggling to make ends meet, the leftovers provide a sensitive way of helping them out. (We will sometimes produce extra large amounts of food so that we can do that.) Our celebrations, when all of the local home churches come together, include a meal, as do our leadership times. We love our "meatings"!

Prayers

Our God is a creative God, and when we learn to follow the Holy Spirit in our times together, it is amazing what happens. Once in Jesus' presence, He shares His heart with us, and as we listen to Him, He draws us closer to Himself, and leads us in the

WHEN YOU COME TOGETHER

direction that He has planned for us. It is as though we are the instruments of the orchestra, the Holy Spirit is the conductor, and as we each play the melody that He has given us individually, He produces a symphony.

I Corinthians 14:26 says that when you come together, each person has a contribution to make. An open time together when everyone can bring what is on their heart is one of the most characteristic things about church in the home. Perhaps a typical meeting (is there such a thing?) might include some worship including songs, scriptures, praise, then maybe a prophecy or picture that someone has with some accompanying discussion, ministry to the needs of those there, sharing of what people have been learning through the week, prayer over an area of the city where we are wanting to start a new church—the possibilities are endless.

Prayer for an individual is precious. Frequently we have them sit in the center and some come and lay hands on them to identify with them. Then we pray around the area of whatever has prompted the prayer. Often people have prophecies or pictures for them or are impressed with a verse of Scripture for them. This kind of prayer can be life changing! For us, the teaching of John Wimber, founder of the Vineyard Church movement has been so helpful. He taught us, "You spell faith, 'R-I-S-K.'" It can be a risk to boldly pray for specific answers for a person, but God wonderfully responds when we step out in faith.

Following the Holy Spirit in our times together is an adventure!

Practical Application:
1). Take times within the group to have different people facilitate/lead the times together.

2). Practice praying conversationally:

•Each one take a turn praying.

•Only pray a sentence or two each, before the next person prays.

124

The church functions as God designed when the Holy Spirit is allowed to freely and completely fill, anoint, gift, and move in and through believers who are assembled together. When He is allowed to fill each believer, and when He is allowed to be in active control of the believers' gatherings, then He will flow in mighty cleansing, empowering, and leading—distributing an abundance of His fruit, gifts, and ministries. We must allow the Holy Spirit, not man, to lead and anoint our times together. It is a group of believers who have experienced His baptism of power, and are being led by Him, who will experience His highest and best.

Nate Krupp, *God's Simple Plan for His Church*

It is native to our particular species (the new creation) to meet in fellowship, in great informality, in caring, in loving, in sharing, in talking to one another. It is native to our species to want to hear about the Lord Jesus Christ . . . from one another.

Gene Edwards, *How to Meet*

Try to envision one of your future participatory services. Here are some of the exciting components you will see:

Individual praise and worship
- Thanksgiving and testimony
- Confession
- Brief periods of silent meditation
- Encouragement and cheer of others
- Original poetry and song
- Intercession
- Sharing of God's lessons learned
- Sharing of needs
- On-the-spot decision-making and commitments

Just imagine...
- The excitement of your people praying for each other every Sunday, and bearing one another's heavy loads
- The enrichment and joy of hearing what God has been teaching different families
- The thrill of seeing former fraidy-cats stand and worship the Lord, praising Him for who He is and what He's done
- The added meaning in knowing that some of the hymns and responsive readings came from the pens of believers sitting around you—or your own
- The delight of having, someday, a congregation full of impassioned and eloquent leaders

James H. Rutz, *The Open Church*

Practical Application:
Read through this section with paper and pencil in hand, and make note of the things you would change in your group if you wanted to rapidly multiply churches.

To our knowledge, here in the West, there are no examples of church planting movements on the scale that we see in the Third World. Therefore, much of our understanding of the principles involved in rapid church multiplication has to come from those who have experienced them elsewhere. There are a number of principles and practices that are common to church planting movements that support the rapid growth that characterizes them. If followed here in the West, I believe they will result in much more rapid growth than we have seen so far. I am indebted to several people who are involved in the leadership of church planting movements for the principles set forth in this section. They come from nations such as India and China and cannot be given the credit due them for security reasons.

1. The importance of vision

If the people in our churches have a vision for rapidly multiplying churches, then they will be looking for ways to implement that vision. One of the churches here in Austin just recently celebrated their one-year anniversary. The couple leading it were so disturbed that they had gone for a year without multiplying out that they decided to disband their church and see what God would do. Out of that group two churches, a prayer time and a group that meets across the churches for fellowship have formed with a third church also planned. But it would not have happened if there were not a vision for growth and multiplication.

Rapid reproduction needs to be a part of the DNA of our churches. Everyone needs to know that they can start a church. We quite often get phone calls from Christians who live locally asking us if they can join one of our churches. Our answer is "We would prefer to help you start one in your home!"

2. Willingness to implement a strategy

If you don't intentionally plan what you are aiming for or praying for in terms of a church-planting

Control is inversely proportional to growth

Quality is not inversely proportional to speed of growth or multiplication

A friend from China

What will the churches that are planted look like? …

They primarily meet in small groups, in many settings operating covertly. They usually have ten to twenty people. They are led by laymen rather than by ordained, professionally educated clergy. The ordinances are conducted by the group; they do not wait for outsiders to come in and assist with ordinances. There is a heavy emphasis on prayer. There is a degree of koinonia, often extending to the point of the sharing of resources – a sharing which extends beyond emotional oneness to oneness in material possessions as well. It is typified by a loose network in which at the very least a church will know its parent group and other churches planted by the parent group. Frequently the churches and the believers are acquainted with suffering. Yet the believers and the churches are characterized by boldness. They do not have dedicated facilities (church buildings). They frequently have women in key roles in the church. Women are viewed as ministers, as having spiritual gifts just as much as men, even in patriarchal societies. (Biblical parallels would include Junia, Phoebe, the four daughters of Philip, Priscilla, Dorcas, Lydia, etc.) The groups are characterized by intentional sharing of the gospel and intentional plans to multiply.   Multiplication is an expectation, not a vague, remote hope.

Finally they recognize that scripture and the Holy Spirit are all they need. They are not heavily dependent upon outside resources but view scripture and the Holy Spirit as adequate for their needs.

A friend from China

The best method under heaven for evangelism is church planting. There never was a better method and there never will be.

Dr. Peter Wagner

movement, someone or something else will take control of the process, whether it's inertia or other individuals. Most often, inertia or tradition will take over, and that is rarely going to take you where you need to go. You will rarely accomplish more or differently than you are aiming for. If you fail to plant churches that have rapid reproduction in their DNA, then you are planning to fail in that regard.

A friend from China

That is no less true in this country. The most likely things that will prevent our churches from becoming part of a church planting movement are inertia—it's just too much trouble and everyone is too busy to get out there and fulfill the Great Commission —or tradition. People who join us from other churches sometimes leave after a few months. The usual reason is the lack of programs for their kids that they had become accustomed to in more traditional churches. Jesus Himself recognized this when He said, "And no one puts new wine into old wineskins. The new wine would burst the old skins, spilling the wine and ruining the skins. New wine must be put into new wineskins. But no one who drinks the old wine seems to want the fresh and the new. 'The old is better,' they say." (Luke 5:37-39) It is interesting that Jesus here has as much concern about the old wineskins as he does about the new wine. And any connoisseur of wine knows that old wine is better. So people who have been brought up in the old church traditions can find it very hard to change. But while they are hankering for the old, it is much more difficult for them to throw their hearts into the new.

Every living thing in God's creation is designed to reproduce. And the church should be no exception. Sterility, or barrenness is repugnant to God. It is not just believers who are to reproduce, but churches.

RAPID MULTIPLICATION

There are four basic ways in which churches can multiply.

1. A community of believers can grow larger to the point where it has to divide into two. Here, the shorter the reproduction time, (6 months is a good length of time), the less likely this is to cause problems for those in the group. A vision of a church planting movement will make this a joyful birth, not a painful divorce.

2. When starting a church in an area or people group where you do not yet know anyone, then a Luke 10 approach can be used (see section 9). From there, other groups will springboard along relational lines.

3. When a new person becomes a believer, an evangelistic discussion group can be started around their circle of family and friends. As more people become disciples, this metamorphoses into a church. (See below)

4. A group of leaders can be trained to go out and start churches, and then train others to do the same (II Timothy 2:2). A strategy coordinator with the Southern Baptists in Cambodia trained six Cambodian leaders over a period of several months. That first year they started six churches. Ten years later, there are over 100,000 new believers.

Some tend to think it is somehow unspiritual to strategize how we can reach our cities for God. But as the saying goes, "If we fail to plan, we plan to fail." If we do not know which the unreached people groups are in our city, and are not actively praying that God will reveal his strategy as to how to reach those groups, then we are unlikely to disciple those groups.

Evaluating how things are going with an open mind to change is another important part of strategizing. Just because "We've always done it that way," is no reason to continue. If we want to see different results to what we have been seeing so far, we will need to change something!

The Marine Warfighting Manual states that risk is inherent equally to action and inaction. This is manifestly untrue in matters of church planting. Inaction has infinitely more risks than action.

A friend from China

Random or haphazard ministry will not produce the same type or quality of fruit that intentional ministry produces in the context of a great vision which glorifies the Lord. One will rarely accomplish better quality fruit or more fruit than is specifically planned for.

A friend from China

3. Immediate baptism

Those who study these things say that the sooner a person is baptized, the less likely they are to fall away. The tendency is to encourage new believers to wait awhile before getting baptized so that they have a chance to be discipled, and then we ask them to get baptized as an act of obedience or witness to their friends and family. But baptism accomplishes something in spiritual realms that we can only dimly perceive. Sometimes it seems that unbelievers understand more in these areas than we do. In many parts of the world, such as India, if people claim to have become Christians, there is really no problem. But let them get baptized and all hell breaks loose! Why? Because something significant has occurred in spiritual realms.

We now encourage whoever leads someone to the Lord to baptize him or her as soon as possible (we have often used a Jacuzzi or bathtub).

4. The resources are in the harvest

Whether it is buildings (homes or places of work or even under a tree) or leadership, finances or manpower, the resources are in the harvest. For example, the person who will end up leading a new simple church a few months from now is very likely not yet a believer. If we have to wait for anything to be imported in from the outside, or if we teach the churches by our own example that they, in themselves, do not have all the resources needed to accomplish everything God wants them to, then we are dramatically slowing down a move of God.

5. Speeding up the process

One of the ways in which we have been most profoundly challenged by the church leaders from China is the sense of urgency with which they work. To them, time is souls passing into a Christless eternity. They say that one of the maxims by which they work is that what they used to do on a monthly basis they

The essence of insanity is to keep doing the same
things over and over expecting different results.

Attributed to Albert Einstein

Often, though not exclusively, the person of peace has the church meet in their home and may
even be the new leader of the emerging church. A church that starts this way is unique in that
it is born out of the harvest, is found among the harvest, and is bent on a mission to continue to
reach the lost. Many house churches suffer from "koinonitis," where fellowship and community
is the main and only thing. What is needed is a strong, healthy dose of mission."

Neil Cole and Paul Kaak, *Organic Church Planting*

If you are working among an unreached people group, the chances are that the greatest church planters, the most effective church planters among your target group in two
years are people who are not yet even believers. The most effective church planters two
years from now will be people who will be won, perhaps, in the next few months. The
resources are truly in the harvest. If we fail to plan for that and fail to recognize that fact,
we are condemning the results to be relatively meager. No unreached people group can
afford to rely primarily on outside workers for evangelism and church planting. Outside
workers are necessary to get a work started; but once it is started, it must be carried out
and carried to completion by members of that target group, or it is destined for failure.

A friend from China

now do weekly, and what they did weekly they now do daily. How can this translate into a western culture where everyone is so busy? Could we be involved in discipling someone on a daily basis for a week or two? If a person had to go to a business conference as a part of their work, they would think that was nothing unusual. Can we not do the same for the Kingdom of God?

6. Begin new churches around new believers

If new believers are added to an existing church, a great opportunity to spread the Gospel is lost. Never at any other stage will they have as many non-Christian friends and family as they do now. So why not teach the new believer how to witness to his friends and family and start a new church around him.

Two other principles factor in here. It is easier to move along existing relationship lines, and it is easier to work with groups rather than individuals. So if a person shows an interest in the Gospel, consider starting a group in their home with their family and friends. It used to be that people would believe in Christianity before they joined the church. In this generation, people want to belong before they believe. So increasingly, we are starting groups among non-believers who love to belong to a relationship-based community. Then over a period of time, both their beliefs and their lifestyle change. Often there is no definitive "moment of salvation." Our limited experience shows that the fallout rate is much lower that way too.

7. The M.A.W.L. principle

This is one of the most important lessons that we have learned from our friends in China. The acronym MAWL stands for model, assist, watch and leave.

1. Model
   If a simple style of church is modeled, new believers can easily reproduce it. (Simple is *not* synonymous with shallow!)

For instance, notice that, if you have a reproduction rate of five years, which is sixty months, over a period of ten years you will end up with only four churches. However, if you could knock this down to a twelve month reproduction rate for a period of ten years, starting with one church, in ten years you would have one thousand twenty-four churches. If you could knock the rate down to a four-month reproduction rate and maintain that for a period of ten years, you would have one billion churches.

A friend from China

The church growth movement has two rules which are true in every society studied. The first rule is that smaller churches grow faster than bigger churches. The second rule is that newer churches grow faster than older churches. This is one good reason to seek to start as many new churches as possible rather than incorporating new converts into existing churches.

A friend from China

At all costs, a new believer or seeker should not be extracted from his social circle into an already existing church until his circle has been evangelized. (The exception to this rule would be an alcoholic or drug user if his social circles would keep him entrapped.) Each new social circle is potentially a new house church: do not alienate the convert from his people.

Dick Scoggins, *Planting House Churches in Networks*

So for example, if you want the churches to have plurality of leadership, then that needs to be modeled to them right from the start. If you want them to learn how to get into the Bible as a group, so that their authority is the Bible rather than a person, then you do not need to be teaching them from the front. Whatever you show them by your life, that is what a group of new believers will tend to copy. When you go into a new situation, you model to them everything that you want that church to be.

2. Assist
Then you need to assist the new church to start another church. You work with the leadership and help them to begin a new church in just the same way that you did with them.

3. Watch
Stage 3 is when you watch your first church plant help their first daughter church to start another church.

4. Leave
This is probably the most difficult step. When you know that the churches can multiply without your aid, then the time has come for you to leave. Obviously you are going to maintain relationship with them, but they are now able to reproduce churches without you and so you are free to go and start churches elsewhere. This approach takes a strong reliance on the Holy Spirit to watch over the new churches.

In church planting it is helpful to keep in mind the training cycle: model, assist, watch, and leave. Generational markers can often serve as a useful guide in knowing when to change roles. That is, the church-planting team model as they plant a church. Then they change roles after the establishment of the church and take an assisting role. They assist the first-generation church in planting a second-generation church. After the second-

The training cycle was used: model, assist, watch, and leave. In general, modeling was done as church planters planted a church. Then a shadow pastor would stay on to assist that church as they planted another church. Then, from a distance, they would watch to ensure that third-generation and repeat second-generation reproduction occurred. Then they would leave and begin work elsewhere.

A friend from China

RAPID MULTIPLICATION

generation church is planted, they again change roles and begin watching as the second-generation church plants a third-generation church with the assistance of the first-generation church. When this takes place, the church-planting team can transition to start work in a new area, modeling again as they do the work in another first-generation church.

A friend from China

About nine months ago a number of our daughter, Becky's, friends in their late teens and early twenties started to find the Lord. It started when she invited a group of her non-Christian friends to come to our house to discuss where they were on their spiritual journeys. Over the next few weeks several of them found the Lord, as shown by dramatic changes in their personal lives and a desire to get baptized (very few "sinner's prayers" here!) This grew into a church which was primarily led by them. So this was our first generation of church where we modeled how church was to be done.

Five months ago we decided that it now needed to move out of our home. One of the young men said that he was willing to start something in his home. The first week, there were around ten new people there that we had never seen before, and one of the girls gave her heart to the Lord. That has continued and goes from strength to strength, our only input being that we meet fairly regularly with those leading it. In this stage we have assisted the first church to start a second one.

Three months ago, one of the new Christians from this church felt that she was able to start something in her home, and so the second generation church assisted her to start a group (we were out of the country at the time and knew nothing about it until our return!) And so now we are at the stage of leaving. We still meet regularly with the leaders to encourage and train them, but we have found that the MAWL model works well.

RAPID MULTIPLICATION

8.   Leadership principles

Once a simple church has been started, it is important to pass on leadership as quickly as possible to local people. This will prevent a church becoming dependent on outsiders. We have learned this lesson the hard way. One of our churches in the projects, for reasons we thought were good at the time, continued to be helped by outside leadership for many months. When, a year later, we felt that that church needed to multiply out by starting a new church with both under local leadership, the daughter church thrived, but the original church felt that they had been abandoned. We had fostered an unhealthy dependence on outside leadership.

One of the church planting movements in China works like this. When a group of seekers come together, they go through a series of eight very simple, daily, evangelistic Bible studies. At the end of the eight days, those that have more interest go on for a series of twelve discipleship studies, again daily. At this point, the new believers are baptized, and leaders that have been identified over the three weeks by their willingness to be totally obedient to what they have been learning are appointed. From that time onwards, all leadership is done through the local leaders, and the outside church-planter mentors or shadow-pastors the new leaders. They will spend time with them teaching them the things that they want that new group to learn and encouraging them in how to look after the new group, and how to start new groups (see the MAWL principle above).

Leadership needs to be composed of ordinary people from the people group that is being discipled. If the new believer feels that he or she needs special training before being qualified to lead, this will become a rate-limiting step in the growth of the new church network. This is something that needs to be modeled from the beginning.

Leadership needs to be plural, teams. The Internet can be a prophetic picture of how leadership functions. The Internet

In any land, when laborers, mechanics, clerks, or truck drivers teach the Bible, lead in prayer, tell what God has done for them, or exhort the brethren, the Christian religion looks and sounds natural to ordinary men. No paid worker from the outside, and certainly no missionary from abroad, can know as much about a neighborhood as someone who has dozens of relatives and intimates all about him. True, on new ground the outsider has to start new expansions. No one else can. But the sooner he turns the churches over to local men, the better.

Dr. Donald McGavran, *Understanding Church Growth*

is a network rather than a hierarchy. There is no single location on the Internet that controls all the information out there. It is similar with team leadership. Where there is a network of churches, there does not need to be a "super-Apostle" in charge, controlling everything that goes on. Rather, a team of interdependent leaders, working with a group of interdependent churches, each with their own strengths and weaknesses can build the whole body together.

9.   Willingness to let it go out of control

Wherever one looks at church planting movements, there is an "out-of-control" aspect to what is going on. That is not to say that there is no structure, but the leadership of it has long since realized that things are moving so fast, there is nothing they can do to keep up with God. They have surrendered it into the hands of the Holy Spirit, and He is doing with it what He wills. This goes against all our natural instincts that make us feel that if we cannot produce numbers, or at least get things into a database, then we are somehow failing. God does not seem too bothered by our inability to keep things ordered!

I long for the day when things are happening at such a pace here in Austin that it is beyond our ability to keep track of everything.

How do you organize a decentralized, rapidly expanding, spontaneous multiplication movement without killing it in the process?

Perhaps the real question is this: can we be out of control and still have order? I believe the answer is *yes*. We can have order in chaos and structure without control, but it must come in a different pattern than what we are accustomed to and emerge from a very different foundation.

Neil Cole

Organization is not a bad thing, but it must be secondary to life and must exist to help support the organic life of the body. Organization can support emerging life, but it can never start it.

Neil Cole

This then is what I mean by spontaneous expansion. I mean the unexhorted and unorganized activity of *individual members of the church* explaining to others the Gospel which they have found for themselves. I mean the expansion which follows the irresistible attraction of the Christian church for those who see its ordered life, and are drawn to it by desire to discover the secret of a life which they instinctively desire to share. I mean also the expansion of the church by the addition of new churches. I know not how it may appear to others, but to me this unexhorted, unorganized, spontaneous expansion has a charm far beyond that of our modern, highly-organized missions.

Roland Allen, *The Spontaneous Expansion of the Church*

PRACTICAL MATTERS

Finances

One of the big advantages to house churches is that they do not have high overheads – no facilities to pay for and maintain, and usually no salaries to provide. Therefore, there is plenty of money to give away to missions or to the poor. We estimate that we give away about 85% of what comes in. The rest goes to things like Bibles, food, and renting a facility when we all come together. It is a huge blessing to be able to be involved in mission situations, especially when some of our people may go to visit and bring back a first hand report of what is happening.

However, one of the potential disadvantages is that finances have such a low profile that many are not encouraged into the spiritual blessings of giving. It is vital that these newly emerging churches cultivate giving as a core value. Giving helps turn our focus from ourselves to others. The American church is already so consumer driven. The last thing we want to see is house churches going along the same self-centered path. Finances provide a wonderful opportunity to demonstrate that our concern is genuinely for the whole world.

An area of stewardship that people often ask about relates to tax deductibility of donations to and through home churches. There is not room in this brief overview of the subject to look at the theological and practical reasons why Christians may have very differing views on the appropriateness of this course of action. Some do not like the idea of "registering" any church with the government. Others see some conflict with a church "using" governmental approaches to save money for their donors. Others feel that the most responsible way to donate money is to make sure that we maximize the tax benefits of our giving in such a way that we can give even more!

There are various ways in which churches can deal with the tax-exempt issue. First, a home church is a real church. It is both legal and ethical for a home church to apply as an individual entity for 501(c)(3) status. Your accountant or attorney

Ten years ago, I asked the Lord a question: "What is the church?" I asked the question partly because of a stirring in my spirit, but also because of the fact that I was part of the leadership of a thousand plus member church with a million dollar a year budget. Although our church and Christian school generated a million a year in income, money was tight. When we didn't have the money to help a member family through a rough time at Christmas (the husband out of work) I said to myself, "There is something wrong with this picture!" Hence the question!

I read the New Testament again, especially the book of Acts, with new eyes…

Ten years later, we still travel the road. We have a network of home churches in central Texas. Because we use 80% of our income for benevolence and missions, we support 10 local ministries and have planted 220 churches in India. Not bad for a small band (about 100) of pioneers!

Jim Mellon, *Ten Years in a House Church*

usually does this. The costs should be under $1000 to set up in the normal course of events. Many house churches, because of their smaller size, choose not to go this route, but via an existing entity, such as the American Evangelistic Association (888-526 3751) or any other Christian entity that acts as an umbrella organization for smaller churches. The cost of setting up will be much lower in this approach, but typically the umbrella organization will take a very small percentage of what you put through their accounts to cover their administration and upkeep.

In Paul's letter to the Colossians he says, "Let the peace of God rule in your hearts." Whether you do or do not use the 501(c)(3) route; let's all keep faithful to the wonderful opportunities that abound for giving through home churches.

Kids

When we tell others that our churches meet in homes, invariably one of the first questions they ask is, "What do you do with the kids?" There are almost as many answers to this question as there are churches, since every situation will vary according to the people involved. In some of our churches, the kids far outnumber the adults. However, as a general rule, our answer is that we include the children in on everything possible.

Let me illustrate by describing the second church meeting we had at a low-income housing project we recently began visiting. The ten adults were outnumbered by about fifteen kids, varying in age from 18 months to 16 years. The majority of these kids had never been to anything like this before. As soon as we arrived, the kids we knew ran out to greet us, wanting to choose a song to sing and trying to teach their favorite ones to their friends. It was chaos! When the meal was over, someone started strumming his guitar, and the kids sang their hearts out. Each wanted to choose their favorite song. "Lord, I Lift Your Name on High" seems to be in the #1 spot!

This means that when the church gathers, the children should be part of the gathering. We know of some groups that purposely direct part of the gathering toward the children: they let them pick out songs to sing, and/or they have a brief teaching directed to them. And, of course, they should be allowed to participate in the gathering just like everyone else. Some of the most precious, insightful words that have been shared in the gatherings have come spontaneously from the children: real words of wisdom and knowledge, prophetic words, teaching, exhortations, "the word of the Lord."

If the gathering gets too lengthy, the parents can excuse their children to go to another room or outside. Sometimes, the Holy Spirit leads someone to have something prepared to do with the children once they are excused.

Nate Krupp, *God's Simple Plan for His Church*

Children are needed to humble us with their questions, break up our endless "adult" discussions, bring us constantly down to earth from our pious clouds, and act as natural evangelists and bridge builders. They also help us to prove the Fruits of the Spirit (eg. patience) and will serve as heaven-sent spies to spot any trace of religious superstition and hypocrisy in us in an instant.

Wolfgang Simson, *Houses That Change the World*

PRACTICAL MATTERS

There was lots of testimony, this time by the adults because we had seen a dramatic healing of one of their relatives during the previous week. Everyone was very excited about this. The kids laid hands on an adult who needed healing. One of the youngest ones, by this time, had fallen asleep on a sofa. When the moment came for us to spend time in discussion around the Bible, a couple of older teens, who come with us because they love church in the projects, went out to play with the kids, while the adults had some time on their own. Initially, there was a bit of traffic in and out, and we had to ask the kids if they would stay outside until we had finished. But eventually they settled down. After it was over, we had several of the younger girls walk us around the complex and introduce us to their friends. This way we had the opportunity to meet a number of other families and invite them to come the next week.

The first time we were there, following a testimony by a teen who has recently started following the Lord, several of the kids (as well as two or three adults) had put their hands up saying that they wanted to follow God too! Typically, the kids take a very active part in the testimony and prayer, as well as the worship and praise. We are asking the Lord that we would see young kids giving prophecies, having visions, etc., but we haven't experienced much in this area yet. During our Bible study time, often someone will have been delegated to take the children out. In some groups the kids prefer to stay in, so we provide toys for them to play with, sitting quietly while the adults are discussing. We do not mind if they are not silent, or if occasionally an adult will need to go and see to a problem. This is family, and children are an integral part!

WHERE DO WE GO FROM HERE?

Your church is growing. Your living room is packed out with adults and kids alike, and new people are coming regularly. Help! What should you do next? There is no right or wrong answer to this question. You will have to seek the Lord for your own situation. However, here are some pointers that, hopefully, will help you to avoid some of the mistakes we have made along the way!

1.   How big should we let our house church get before we encourage it to multiply?

The experts claim that 15-20 adults is the maximum number that you should let a house church grow to. Although we have had them grow to 40 or more, a group this large loses the sense of intimacy, and it becomes more difficult for everyone to participate.

2.   How do we divide our house church?

The first church we started in Austin grew to around 50 before we split it into two. For a year after that, people would say to us that it was like having gone through a divorce. So, we no longer multiply by dividing a church into two. Before the group gets too large, we try to send out one or two couples and/or singles to birth a daughter church. When we think our numbers are reaching a maximum point, if a new family wants to join, rather than include them in the existing church, we will try to start a new church around them. Normally, we will draw on one of the families from the existing church. That way it is an exciting church plant that the original group takes ownership of and will support. It also typically has the advantage of moving into a new neighborhood, with a new set of people getting involved.

Just recently, we started a new church this way. The parents of one of our daughter's friends wanted to join us, so we asked a number of other parents of her friends to come, plus some other newcomers. BINGO! A new church has started. It began in our house, but within six weeks moved into one of their homes.

Size is the real issue. The church should be relational, personal, intimate, and committed. It should be like a family. The Bible uses family terms to describe our relationships to God and each other (father, mother, brothers, sisters, son, daughter, child). Size definitely affects a group's relationships. Social scientists have shown that smaller groups encourage more participation, closer interaction, more accountability, and closer relationships. This is nothing new. Our Lord worked with only twelve men that He could build into a community. Spiritual growth happens best in an intimate environment. This needs face-to-face accountability, which depends on size.

Because a house church is small, people develop meaningful relationships more easily. This encourages each person to take part in all the chores. There are no observers in a household. In a house church, not only do members observe and receive instruction but everyone actively participates in the ministry of the church. The church in the home fosters a high level of commitment. Participants either become significantly involved or they drop out quickly. The house church fosters mutual commitment. People minister to each other concerning everyday problems: family members examine how the Bible speaks to their everyday concerns. The Bible is our authority as we deal with real life situations in a caring family environment. Some of our meetings look like family "pow wows" around the dinner table where we discuss the day's problems and look for solutions.

Dick Scoggins, *Planting House Churches in Networks*

3. Should our churches have outside input?

The answer to this question is a definite "Yes!" It is very easy for small groups to become isolated and insular. At that point, they tend to become inward looking. Over the years, we have found that outside input has been invaluable. The church is built on the foundation of apostles and prophets, and that principle needs to have a practical application for us as churches.

We would advise every church to make sure that it is regularly inviting in Ephesians 4 type ministries to help keep the focus outwards and the vision expanding. As networks of churches emerge in one local area, it is also likely that the different churches will develop different emphases and goals. This is good. But to maintain the sense of unity, it is also good to continue to meet from time to time for celebration worship. This also allows input from the apostolic and prophetic voices that are growing up within the churches or that are visiting from other regions.

4. What about elders and deacons?

You've started a house church. In fact, you've started several house churches, and now you start to think about leadership of this emerging network. Isn't it time to appoint elders and deacons? How should you handle it? The foundations that you lay are so important—they can never be laid again a second time.

It is for this reason, and because the Scriptures are not totally clear on the subject, that our personal preference is not to go with New Testament titles at this point. Let me illustrate. Acts 14:23 describes how Paul and Barnabus return to the churches that they had started some months previously, and "appoint elders in every church, turning them over to the care of the Lord in whom they had come to trust." The church in any given city met primarily in homes, even if they also met publicly as they did in Ephesus. What is not clear is whether Paul appointed elders in every church that met in a home, or if it was in the church in the city, which might

Practical Application:
Does our group already have outside links that we can develop into stronger realtionships?

Are we as a group encouraging our own members to use their giftings to be a blessing to other churches?

Church planting does not necessarily have to take place via apostles—all believers may plant legitimate churches. Still, any church will benefit by being relationally engaged with apostolic teams.

Robert Lund, *The Way Church Ought To Be*

WHERE DO WE GO FROM HERE?

have met in a number of homes. However, it becomes clearer in Titus 1:5, where Titus is instructed to appoint elders in every city. There is no example in the New Testament of an elder being described as associated with a church in a home. The examples we have are of elders in the church in a city, for example, in Jerusalem. What if we appoint elders in each home church now, only a few years down the line to find that God is revealing the importance of city church and all the elders have to be demoted!

What are important however, are the principles of leadership. In general, the church appoints people into positions of responsibility because they can perform well in public. The New Testament knows little of this. Repeatedly, the New Testament talks of leadership in terms of service, caring for people, laying down one's life for them. Leadership is by example. The qualifications for eldership in the passages in I Timothy and Titus, describe character issues, not charisma. A leader is to be hospitable and able to teach. He must have a good reputation in the world. He is to be faithful to his wife, not a drunkard or violent, but gentle. He must manage his own family well. The same is true when talking of deacons. In Acts 6, the deacons who were chosen were "well respected, full of the Holy Spirit and wisdom. The term "presbuteros," which is translated "elder", literally means "an older man" and his function was to watch over rather than control.

So our personal preference is that the churches meet in various homes or other locations where they are usually, but not always, the responsibility of the person whose home it is in, or the person who started it. These may be very young Christians, the persons of peace, who are being mentored in their role by someone who has been a Christian for longer. The overall leadership of the network, however, needs to be of the kind of caliber that we are talking about in the paragraph above.

155

5. What about the role of apostles and prophets?

The ministries mentioned in Ephesians 4, apostles, prophets, evangelists, pastors and teachers, are people whose ministry may be trans-local, i.e., they have influence and ministry beyond their own church. Their role is to equip the saints for the work of ministry. In contemporary Christian culture, when a visiting ministry comes into town it is often an excuse for them to showcase their gifts. But according to Ephesians 4, the apostle's work is that of equipping the saints to plant churches, the prophets should be teaching people how to prophesy, etc. These ministries have all the gifts necessary to equip the local people to take their cities for Christ and to plant communities of His people everywhere! And we need to take every opportunity that we can to learn from them.

Unfortunately, the terms have often been hijacked. Having the title of "Apostle" or "Prophet" on a business card has little to do with the real thing! Sadly, those who are just trying to build their own empires or extend their own spheres of influence are using the term and bringing it into disrepute. For the genuine item, look at Paul's description of his apostleship in I Corinthians 4:9-16. As Wolfgang Simson says, the apostles should be weeping fathers who are longing for their children to overtake them.

We need to find those with the heart of a true apostle and learn from them.

6. Should all the churches meet together regularly?

This is a question that we are currently looking at. For the past several years, ever since our first house church divided into two, we have had a monthly celebration. These have been great, and they are a wonderful forum for outside ministries to come in and equip the whole body. However, as we continue to grow and need ever larger facilities for the celebration, we are trying to decide between three options:

My own view is one that stresses relationship over covering. It is about being a father to those who are setting out with a vision the Lord has placed in them. As a spiritual father, I come alongside to assist and to give and to support, and not interfere and not demand certain things. I believe fathering means exercising influence through intimate relationship and a desire to follow the heart of the Father as Jesus demonstrated. I must live likewise, and continue to exhort and encourage and counsel through the means of relationship, those whom the Lord has given me to father and care for. As a father I am called to bring to maturity those very same church planters, so that they will be able to stand and be able to move in their calling and destiny. When I father them in this way, then I am fulfilling my apostolic mandate. Being apostolic means weeping and interceding, and pouring your life for the sake of others and the Body. Too much of what is spoken of as apostolic today does not have these characteristics and that really bothers me.

Sam Buick

section fourteen

WHERE DO WE GO FROM HERE?

Practical Application:
This group is nearing the end of these study materials. Here are some questions that need answering in order to move on:

1). What are we doing to grow from one group into a network of house churches?

2). Are there people outside the group whose insight and encouragement we appreciate that we should be asking for help as we pray towards growth?

3). How can we develop links with other like-minded groups locally?

1. Should we continue to meet all together monthly, which everyone loves and appreciates?

2. Should we only meet periodically when someone with apostolic or prophetic gifting comes through town, and meet in our house churches the rest of the time?

3. Should we develop a series of mini-celebrations around the city, with groups of churches getting together, while on occasion, maybe quarterly, having a major celebration with everyone involved? This last approach would have the added advantage of training some people up into leadership of a larger gathering. It would also help relieve the host families of the many home churches on a monthly basis.

The questions surrounding the importance of networking the networks, having conferences, or providing an international missions thrust are quite numerous. Exploring these areas will challenge emerging house church networks to grow and mature.

159

JESUS, BUILD YOUR CHURCH!

As these house church networks increase in number, there are some principles that we at House2House feel should characterize what is happening. A year ago, the Lord gave me a sort of triple slogan that we try to live by: "*No empire building, no control, and no glory*."

No empire building

Our focus needs to be on building the Kingdom of God, not our own kingdoms. It is so easy, as a work of God grows, for a person to think he is the indispensable leader and to take the position of a CEO—the one who, like Saul, is head and shoulders above the others. The history of the church is riddled with men claiming ownership of God's work. There will be people who become more well known in what God is doing, but let us pray that these are people walking with a limp, who know what it is to wrestle with God and for God to have won (see the story of when Jacob wrestled with the Lord in Genesis 32). They should care more about God's Kingdom than their own reputation. May those who rise to prominence be ones who are dead to their own desires for power, and who long for God to be glorified above all. Let them be weeping fathers who seek God—fathers and mothers who desire that their sons and daughters overtake them. Only those with a heart such as this can be trusted to lead a movement of God!

No control

There is a huge temptation to try and control what is going on, often with the best of intentions. However, we need to understand who the head of the church is, and decide whether or not we are willing to risk letting the Holy Spirit direct things. Paul must have faced this many times. He would sometimes have to leave a church after days or weeks (e.g., Philippi, Thessalonica or Berea), and he would have to trust the ongoing growth of the new believers to the Holy Spirit.

A true and safe leader is one who has no desire to lead, but is forced into a position of leadership by the Holy Spirit and external situations. A reliable rule of thumb is as follows: A man who is ambitious to lead is disqualified as a leader. A true leader will have no desire to lord it over God's heritage. He is rather ready to follow as well as lead.

A. W. Tozer, *The Reaper*

I feel comfortable releasing control of disciples, leaders, churches and movements as long as I know that each unit is connected to the Master. This is as it should be.

Neil Cole

JESUS, BUILD YOUR CHURCH!

We faced a paradigm shift in our thinking on this subject that we call our "Cornelius experience." When Cornelius was filled with the Holy Spirit, Peter had a revelation that, contrary to everything he had believed up until that time, God wanted the Gentiles to be part of His Kingdom too.

A couple came over for a meal shortly after we met them in one of our meetings. In the middle of supper, they announced that they were starting their own home church the next Sunday. It sounded like a dozen people were already invited and most had committed to coming!

If they had given us a little more notice, we could have suggested that they maybe come along for a month or two, until they had more understanding of what house church was about, or that maybe they could go through some kind of leaders' training. As it was, we blessed them, prayed for them and offered to help in any way we could. They had about 10 non-Christians at that first meeting with a dozen or so kids. A few months later, several were baptized. Our revelation was that Jesus is building His church, and it is better when we are out of the picture!

We could so easily have gotten in the way of what God was doing by trying to take control. Our motives would have been that we wanted them to church plant in the best way possible. But who is the head of the church? Can we trust other people to let Jesus lead them without interference from us?

No glory

In Isaiah 42:8 it says, "I am the Lord. That is my name. My glory I give to none other." The temptation to take just a little bit of the credit is very strong! It is an incredible privilege to be a part of a move of God, and we need to stay humble.

An example from our life in London should serve as a warning. We were part of a move of God's Spirit back in the 70's. Thou-

162

In the final analysis, to be subject to the headship of Jesus means to obey His will regarding the life and practice of the church . . . Submission to the headship of Christ incarnates the New Testament teaching that Jesus is not only Lord of the lives of men, but that He is Master of the life of the church. And Scripture is plain that when Christ's headship is established and given concrete expression in the earth, He will become head over all things in the universe (Col 1:16-18).

Frank Viola, *Rethinking the Wineskin*

Never in the New Testament is one believer, even a church leader, said to have spiritual authority over another. Christians have authority over things, and even over spirits, but not over other Christians.

Christian Smith, *Going to the Root*

JESUS, BUILD YOUR CHURCH!

sands of churches started in homes all over the country, but, usually, they very quickly grew to be the largest church in town. Ours was no exception. In just a few years we had grown to several hundred, and there was an incredible sense of the presence of God in our meetings.

One day, Tony overheard two people talking after a meeting. They were commenting on how glad they were to be part of this church, rather than another church that they named. They talked about how much better this church was, and how much God was moving with us compared to other churches in the area. Tony knew that what they were saying was wrong, and yet in his heart he agreed with them. It was just a reflection of the arrogance that had crept in. Within a few months, the Lord allowed our church to be split down the middle in a very painful way. As we sought the Lord as to why this had happened, we felt clear that God was dealing with our pride. He could not trust us if we had that kind of attitude. We dare not risk trying to take any glory for ourselves, or thinking that we are better than others.

God can only trust us if we make sure that all the glory goes to Him. He wants this to be a grassroots church planting movement of ordinary people that does not rely on big names. The only superstar in what is going on needs to be the Lord Jesus.

Practical Application:
When and where is the Lord asking me to start a church?

Who can start a church? You can! If God is leading you in this way, you do not need anyone's permission before going ahead. Obviously, you would do well to seek the input of other like-minded people and to learn all that you can from the increasing amount of material that is out there. But if God is leading you, go ahead. The wave is coming in. You are in for the ride of a lifetime!

You have a Bible? You can read? Then you can start a church!

Indian church planter

RESOURCES

Books

Missionary Methods	Roland Allen
The Church Comes Home	Robert and Julia Banks
Simply Church	Tony and Felicity Dale
How to Meet	Gene Edwards
The Church in the House	Robert Fitts
Saturation Church Planting	Robert Fitts
Church Planting Movements	David Garrison
The Naked Church	Wayne Jacobsen
House Church Networks	Larry Kreider
God's Simple Plan for His Church	Nate Krupp
The Way Church Ought to Be	Robert Lund
The Open Church	James Rutz
Houses that Change the World	Wolfgang Simson
Rethinking the Wineskin	Frank Viola

Magazine

House2House Magazine
(512) 282-2322 or www.house2house.tv to subscribe

Videos

Church Planting Movements - www.imb.org

Mark 9:50
Salt is good, but if the salt loses its flavor, how will you season it? Have salt in yourselves, and have peace with one another.

John 13:14
If I then, your Lord and Teacher, have washed your feet, you also ought to wash one another's feet.

John 13:34
A new commandment I give to you, that you love one another; as I have loved you, that you also love one another.

John 13:35
By this all will know that you are My disciples, if you have love for one another.

John 15:12
This is My commandment, that you love one another as I have loved you.

John 15:17
These things I command you, that you love one another.

Romans 12:5
 . . . So we, being many, are one body in Christ, and individually members of one another.

Romans 12:10
Be kindly affectionate to one another with brotherly love, in honor giving preference to one another;

Romans 12:16
Be of the same mind toward one another. Do not set your mind on high things, but associate with the humble. Do not be wise in your own opinion.

Romans 13:8
Owe no one anything except to love one another, for he who loves another has fulfilled the law.

Romans 14:13
Therefore let us not judge one another anymore, but rather resolve this, not to put a stumbling block or a cause to fall in our brother's way.

Romans 14:19
Therefore let us pursue the things which make for peace and the things by which one may edify another.

Romans 15:5
Now may the God of patience and comfort grant you to be like-minded toward one another, according to Christ Jesus,

Romans 15:7
Therefore receive one another, just as Christ also received us, to the glory of God.

Romans 15:14
Now I myself am confident concerning you, my brethren, that you also are full of goodness, filled with all knowledge, able also to admonish one another.

Romans 16:16
Greet one another with a holy kiss. The churches of Christ greet you.

1 Corinthians 6:7
Now therefore, it is already an utter failure for you that you go to law against one another. Why do you not rather accept wrong? Why do you not rather let yourselves be cheated?

1 Corinthians 10:24
Let no one seek his own, but each one the other's well-being.

1 Corinthians 11:33
Therefore, my brethren, when you come together to eat, wait for one another.

1 Corinthians 12:25
. . . That there should be no schism in the body, but that the members should have the same care for one another . . .

1 Corinthians 16:20
All the brethren greet you. Greet one another with a holy kiss.

2 Corinthians 13:12
Greet one another with a holy kiss.

Galatians 5:13
For you, brethren, have been called to liberty; only do not use liberty as an opportunity for the flesh, but through love serve one another.

Galatians 5:26
Let us not become conceited, provoking one another, envying one another.

Galatians 6:2
Bear one another's burdens, and so fulfill the law of Christ.

Ephesians 4:2
. . . With all lowliness and gentleness, with longsuffering, bearing with one another in love,

Ephesians 4:25
Therefore, putting away lying, let each one of you speak truth with his neighbor, for we are members of one another.

Ephesians 4:32
And be kind to one another, tenderhearted, forgiving one another, just as God in Christ forgave you.

Ephesians 5:19
. . . Speaking to one another in psalms and hymns and spiritual songs, singing and making melody in your heart to the Lord,

Ephesians 5:21
. . . Submitting to one another in the fear of God

Colossians 3:9
Do not lie to one another, since you have put off the old man with his deeds,

Colossians 3:13
. . . Bearing with one another, and forgiving one another, if anyone has a complaint against another; even as Christ forgave you, so you also must do.

Colossians 3:16
Let the word of Christ dwell in you richly in all wisdom, teaching and admonishing one another in psalms and hymns and spiritual songs, singing with grace in your hearts to the Lord.

1 Thessalonians 3:12
And may the Lord make you increase and abound in love to one another and to all, just as we do to you,

1 Thessalonians 4:9
But concerning brotherly love you have no need that I should write to you, for you yourselves are taught by God to love one another;

1 Thessalonians 4:18
Therefore comfort one another with these words.

1 Thessalonians 5:11
Therefore comfort each other and edify one another, just as you also are doing.

Hebrews 3:13
. . . But exhort one another daily, while it is called "Today," lest any of you be hardened through the deceitfulness of sin.

Hebrews 10:24
And let us consider one another in order to stir up love and good works,

Hebrews 10:25
. . . Not forsaking the assembling of ourselves together, as is the manner of some, but exhorting one another, and so much the more as you see the Day approaching.

James 4:11
Do not speak evil of one another, brethren. He who speaks evil of a brother and judges his brother, speaks evil of the law and judges the law. But if you judge the law, you are not a doer of the law but a judge.

James 5:9
Do not grumble against one another, brethren, lest you be condemned. Behold, the Judge is standing at the door!

James 5:16
Confess your trespasses to one another, and pray for one another, that you may be healed. The effective, fervent prayer of a righteous man avails much.

1 Peter 1:22
Since you have purified your souls in obeying the truth through the Spirit in sincere love of the brethren, love one another fervently with a pure heart

The following are some verses that I use all the time in spiritual warfare. I recommend memorizing some of them so that they are useful weapons in our hands against the enemy:

Ephesians 6:10-18
Finally, my brethren, be strong in the Lord and in the power of His might. Put on the whole armor of God, that you may be able to stand against the wiles of the devil. For we do not wrestle against flesh and blood, but against principalities, against powers, against the rulers of the darkness of this age, against spiritual hosts of wickedness in the heavenly places. Therefore take up the whole armor of God, that you may be able to withstand in the evil day, and having done all, to stand. Stand therefore, having girded your waist with truth, having put on the breastplate of righteousness, and having shod your feet with the preparation of the gospel of peace; above all, taking the shield of faith with which you will be able to quench all the fiery darts of the wicked one. And take the helmet of salvation, and the sword of the Spirit, which is the word of God; praying always with all prayer and supplication in the Spirit, being watchful to this end with all perseverance and supplication for all the saints.

II Corinthians 10:3-5
For though we walk in the flesh, we do not war according to the flesh. For the weapons of our warfare are not carnal but mighty in God for pulling down strongholds, casting down arguments and every high thing that exalts itself against the knowledge of God, bringing every thought into captivity to the obedience of Christ,

Matthew 4:1-11
Then Jesus was led up by the Spirit into the wilderness to be tempted by the devil. And when He had fasted forty days and forty nights, afterward He was hungry. Now when the tempter came to Him, he said, "If You are the Son of God, command that these stones become bread." But He answered and said, "It is written, 'Man shall not live by bread alone, but by every word that proceeds from the mouth of God.'" Then the devil took Him up into the holy city, set Him on the pinnacle of the temple, and said to Him, "If You are the Son of God, throw Yourself down. For it is written: 'He shall give His angels charge over you,' and, 'In their hands they shall bear you up, Lest you dash your foot against a stone.'" Jesus said to him, "It is written again, 'You shall not tempt the Lord your God.'" Again, the devil took Him up on an exceedingly high mountain, and showed Him all the kingdoms of the world and their glory. And he said to Him, "All these things I will give You if You will fall down and worship me." Then Jesus said to him, "Away with you, Satan! For it is written, 'You shall worship the Lord your God, and Him only you shall serve.'" Then the devil left Him, and behold, angels came and ministered to Him.

Psalm 149:6-9
Let the high praises of God be in their mouth, And a two-edged sword in their hand, To execute vengeance on the nations, And punishments on the peoples; To bind their kings with chains, And their nobles with fetters of iron; To execute on them the written judgment.

Luke 10:17-20
Then the seventy returned with joy, saying, "Lord, even the demons are subject to us in Your name." And He said to them, "I saw Satan fall like lightning from heaven. Behold, I give you the authority to trample on serpents and scorpions, and over all the power of the enemy, and nothing shall by any means hurt you. Nevertheless do not rejoice in this, that

the spirits are subject to you, but rather rejoice because your names are written in heaven."

John 10:10
The thief does not come except to steal, and to kill, and to destroy. I have come that they may have life, and that they may have it more abundantly.

Acts 10:38
. . . How God anointed Jesus of Nazareth with the Holy Spirit and with power, who went about doing good, and healing all who were oppressed by the devil, for God was with Him.

Colossians 2:14-15
. . . Having wiped out the handwriting of requirements that was against us, which was contrary to us. And He has taken it out of the way, having nailed it to the cross. Having disarmed principalities and powers, He made a public spectacle of them, triumphing over them in it.

James 4:7
Therefore submit to God. Resist the devil and he will flee from you.

I John 4:4
You are of God, little children, and have overcome them, because He who is in you is greater than he who is in the world.

Philippians 2:9-11
Therefore God also has highly exalted Him and given Him the name which is above every name, that at the name of Jesus every knee should bow, of those in heaven, and of those on earth, and of those under the earth, and that every tongue should confess that Jesus Christ is Lord, to the glory of God the Father.

Ephesians 1:20-23, 2:6
. . . Which He worked in Christ when He raised Him from the dead and seated Him at His right hand in the heavenly places, far above all principality and power and might and dominion, and every name that is named, not only in this age but also in that which is to come. And He put all things under His feet, and gave Him to be head over all things to the church, which is His body, the fullness of Him who fills all in all . . . and raised us up together, and made us sit together in the heavenly places in Christ Jesus.

Acts 2:34-35
For David did not ascend into the heavens, but he says himself: "The Lord said to my Lord, 'Sit at My right hand, Till I make Your enemies Your footstool.'"

Hebrews 2:14-15
Inasmuch then as the children have partaken of flesh and blood, He Himself likewise shared in the same, that through death He might destroy him who had the power of death, that is, the devil, and release those who through fear of death were all their lifetime subject to bondage.

Revelation 12:10-12
Then I heard a loud voice saying in heaven, "Now salvation, and strength, and the kingdom of our God, and the power of His Christ have come, for the accuser of our brethren, who accused them before our God day and night, has been cast down. And they overcame him by the blood of the Lamb and by the word of their testimony, and they did not love their lives to the death.

I John 3:8
For this purpose the Son of God was manifested, that He might destroy the works of the devil.

Training the Trainers

WHY TRAINING THE TRAINERS?

Continuing to arrive in the House2House office from all over the country are the stories of how God is leading people to start churches. Whether in homes, offices, hospitals, coffee houses or factories, they are spontaneously springing up all over the nation. The term "house church" is becoming a buzzword that stirs interest among Christians everywhere, whatever their background. Even the secular media are beginning to sit up and take notice! The church "outside the walls" is beginning to have an impact!

The *Getting Started* manual was produced as a result of all the requests for help that the staff at House2House were getting from people asking how they should go about starting a church. Since there was no way that we could adequately respond personally to the volume of calls and emails we were receiving, we decided to produce some written materials. Originally it had a working title of "*Getting Started Right*"; we quickly changed it to just "*Getting Started*," since the last thing we wanted to do was to convey the impression that we somehow had all the answers.

Meanwhile, around the same time here in Austin, we were sensing a real need to train others to start churches too. So we began a church planters' training course called *Luke 10*. Based on a concept that Wolfgang Simson pioneered in Germany and Switzerland, we found ourselves primarily using the materials that we had produced for *Getting Started*. Then came the question, "How do we spread what we have been learning through *Luke 10* to other areas of the country?" Since *Luke 10* here in Austin is run as a series of weekend conferences, it is not really feasible to have people come from all over the country. So came the idea of "*Training the Trainers*."

The concept behind *Training the Trainers* is to enable people to use the materials in the *Getting Started* manual to train groups of people to go out and start networks of churches. It also covers in more depth some of the practical areas that arise as a network of house churches develops. Again, we are not presuming to have all the answers. All of us are in the position of needing to hear from God concerning our own local situations and the last thing we want or need is some kind of cookie cutter approach. But hopefully there are some principles that we have learned over the years that may be of help to some.

Getting Started can be used by the youngest Christians. Anyone can start a church in his home or place of work. We have some youth who are running church, having only been following the Lord for a matter of three months or so. *Training the Trainers*, on the other hand, is designed for those who have a calling to go out and reproduce churches. Does a person

Practical Application:
To see if a *Luke 10* course is planned in the near future, go to the www.house2house.tv website and look under the "Events" page.

Practical Application:
Two to three times a year, we run a Luke 10 course for trainers who will take it to their own areas. If you are already involved in starting churches, and are interested, contact us at www.house2house.tv

have to already had experience in starting house churches before they are qualified to go out and train others to do the same? There's no doubt that having actually done it helps hugely because it adds credibility and because you are speaking from experience and not just head knowledge. But, knowing the Holy Spirit, for some their first experience of house church may be gathering a group together to learn from the materials!

WHAT IS LUKE 10?

All over the world, God is advancing His Kingdom by means of spontaneous, lay led, church planting movements. The purpose of the *Luke 10* course is to equip and train ordinary people to go out and start churches.

- We ran our *Luke 10* course as a series of six weekend conferences over a three-month period, effectively every other weekend. People seemed to cope with this format.

- At a logistical level, we started with a meal together on a Friday evening, and went through until Saturday mid-afternoon. The group was deliberately kept small so that it could be very interactive, and wherever possible, it was made extremely practical.

- Costs were kept to a minimum. People from out of town were accommodated in others' homes. We had an extremely gifted teenager from one of our churches cater the Friday evening and Saturday lunchtime meals which quickly became something of a high spot of our times together!

- Rather than have a specific cost for the course, which might have prevented some key people from joining us, we followed Wolfgang's idea of suggesting people tithe into *Luke 10* for the duration of our time together. We wondered if that would turn some people off, but it seemed to work well. Some paid nothing, while others paid a considerable amount.

- The atmosphere was low-key. Close relationships developed. And every week the Holy Spirit moved powerfully in our midst. Often, our plans would have to change because the Holy Spirit came in and did something different to what we had anticipated, and He was allowed free reign among us.

The following is a brief description of what we covered:

LUKE 10 SCHEDULE

Weekend 1

Friday evening

Start with meal

Teaching on the big picture—stories of house church movements throughout the world (section 3 of *Getting Started*)

Divide down into house churches i.e., groups of 10 to 12 people. Study Acts 13: 1-4, using Bible study method 2 (section 11 of *Getting Started*). Bring out principles of how God leads, plurality of leadership, prophets etc.

Brief session on how to hear God—then divide into pairs and prophesy over each other.

Training the Trainers

Saturday morning

Worship and hearing from God

Teaching on what is church? (Section 4 of *Getting Started*)

3 types of churches -universal, city and house

Divide into house churches. Study Acts 2:41-47 looking at what happens in house church—using an interactive approach (see section 11).

Divide down into Life Transformation Groups as model of accountability group (groups of 2 to 3 using the materials from Church Multiplication Associates—see section 10 of *Getting Started*)

Lunch

Church Planting Movements video (Available from Southern Baptists. www.imb.org and then go to their resources section)

Weekend 2

Friday evening

Meal

Teaching on spiritual warfare and prayer walking (section 7 of *Getting Started*)

Group activity: spend time in aggressive praise, prayer and warfare. We suggest praying together out loud simultaneously. (Acts 4:24 "Then all the believers were united as they lifted their voices in prayer.")

Saturday morning

Worship and hearing from God

Teaching on the Great Omission (section 6 of *Getting Started*)

Group activity: Leading someone to Christ. Discussion about not using religious jargon and keeping it simple. Divide down into pairs and make everyone lead their partner to Christ in 2 minutes without any Christianese

Discussion on baptism and discipleship

Lunch

How to lead someone into the baptism in the Holy Spirit.

Weekend 3

Friday evening

Meal

Aggressive prayer and warfare

Ways of starting house church (section 8 of *Getting Started*). This could be done as a testimony time of how people there have started house churches

Group discussion on how each person would naturally start house church (e.g. with their kids, at work, etc.) with the emphasis on reaching the non-believer.

Saturday morning

Worship and hearing from God

Divide into house churches and do an interactive Bible study on I Corinthians 9:19-23

Teaching on Luke 10 (section 9 of *Getting Started*)

Brief teaching and then group activity on praying for the sick

Brief teaching then group activity on praying for deliverance

Lunch

Teaching on how to see when the Holy Spirit is working

LTG

Weekend 4

Friday evening

Meal

When you come together (section 11 of *Getting Started*)

House church activity - Bible study on I Corinthians 14:26 to end of chapter

Small group dynamics - How to facilitate or steer a meeting

Saturday morning

Teaching on how to hear the Holy Spirit in a meeting and use of gifts of Holy Spirit

Group activity - divide into small groups getting each member of the group to study on their own a different Psalm of Ascent (Psalm 120-134) looking at how to enter God's presence, and share these with the group.

Open meeting putting into practice principles of I Corinthians 14

Lunch

Discussion about leadership and authority

Weekend 5

We invited in someone who has a powerful prophetic ministry and who is working in church planting. I would suggest that it is good to try and get in an outside person who has experience in church planting for a weekend somewhere in the course. You should also cover the material on DNA & Rapid Multiplication (sections 5 and 12).

Weekend 6

Friday night

Meal

Teaching on principles of inner healing

Divide into small groups and pray for one another's needs

Saturday morning

Finances: discussion on how to handle finances in house church context (section 13 of *Getting Started*). Explain the financial situation of the Luke 10 course - how much money came in, expenses incurred etc. Make a group decision as to what to do with the remainder.

Where do we go from here? (section 14 in *Getting Started*) Where is each one who has attended the course going to go with what they have learned? Prayer and waiting on the Lord

Ministry and prayer for each other. Sending out

Lunch

Church Planting Movements video

Final challange to actually do what everyone has been learning

The above was our projected schedule. In practice, the LTG groups generally did not happen through lack of time, but otherwise all the material was covered. After lunch on Saturdays was basically kept for whatever the Holy Spirit was emphasizing. Throughout, the Holy Spirit was welcome to break in and change the schedule, which He frequently did! There was much ministry to individuals (also used as a teaching tool).

It is obvious from the timetable that there was quite an emphasis on prophecy. Some of this was deliberate—some the Holy Spirit added in the form of ministry from outside. **"Programs are what happens when the Holy Spirit does not lead," (Wolfgang Simson).** It is vital in our churches that we know how to recognize the Holy Spirit and to follow His leadings.

KEYS TO LUKE 10 COURSE

The following are some pointers to help make the course as effective as possible

Like house church

We tried to make the atmosphere as much like house church as possible. It was held in a home; it was kept extremely informal; we broke down into small groups as much as possible, usually at a house church sort of size. There was lots of fellowship over meals. Because everything in house church needs to be easily modeled and reproduced, our worship was not preplanned, but spontaneous. The one thing that was not like house church was that there was more teaching from the front. Because of time constraints, this was unavoidable, but even there, people were free to interrupt and often a teaching time would be broken up by spontaneous discussion.

Everything that went on was used as a teaching tool

We tried to make sure that everything was used as a teaching tool. So, for example, if a meeting went in a certain direction we would try to explain why it had gone in that direction. Why did we lead in the way that we did? Why did we break down into ministry at this point rather than waiting until later? How do we hear the Holy Spirit? Why did we move into warfare? Wherever possible, what went on was used to teach house church principles.

Following the Holy Spirit

Although we had a preplanned agenda for each session, the Holy Spirit was free to break in whenever He chose (which was frequently!) Again, our times in the course needed to model how church would run. So if it seemed that the Holy Spirit wanted us to spend more time than we had planned just waiting on the Lord and hearing from Him in prophecy or visions, we would do that even though it might mean that some of the teaching had to be briefer. Or if we sensed a situation required ministry, that need might take precedence over our plans and again would be used to demonstrate how to minister in a house church setting.

Practical

The course was made as practical as possible, and skills learned were reinforced whenever possible. If a subject was taught that had a practical application, then we would make sure that we practiced right there and then. For example, after the session on spiritual warfare, a considerable amount of time was spent in prolonged aggressive praise and warfare, and that was repeated on subsequent weeks. By the end of the course, it was perfectly natural for a prayer time to become a time when all were on our feet, some pacing the room, crying out to God in unison and storming heaven. The presence of God was awesome!

Variety

The sessions were made as varied as possible. If a subject could be taught by means of interactive Bible study, we preferred to do it that way. We tried to never be boring. (You would have to ask someone who attended if we succeeded in that!) There was plenty of time for fellowship and sharing over the meal times, and always people stayed on to chat afterwards. The teaching times were always illustrated with lots of stories.

Comments following the completion of the course indicated that it had been a very significant time in the lives of those present. Hopefully, many churches will be started as a result.

Printed in the United Kingdom
by Lightning Source UK Ltd.
102643UKS00001B/87

9 780971 804036